PRAISE FOR *GROUNDED*

"There was a time in Western civilization when women were the keepers of a sacred trust: humanity's deep connection to the natural world. They held aloft our sense of divine relationship to the earth, the waters, and the sky. With the destruction of pagan culture, the sacred power of such women all but disappeared. What they represented is reappearing now—not a moment too soon—and Erin McMorrow is a proud and worthy daughter to their ancient legacy. Ageless voices seem to be reaching across the years to speak to her, delivering an eternal passion for reconnecting all of us to the divine, to each other, and to the earth on which we live."

MARIANNE WILLIAMSON four-time #1
New York Times bestselling author

"To me, people working on ecosystem science and soil carbon are planetary rock stars in the making! Their work may be critical to people's long-term symbiotic relationship with the earth system—and each other—in more ways than one may initially realize. Humbly, the interconnected and healing world of soil and the carbon cycle that Erin McMorrow gives new insights to couldn't come at a more critical time."

DAVID ADDISON Virgin Group, cofounder of
the nonprofit UK Carbon Removal Centre

"McMorrow takes us along a personal journey in which her most powerful teachers—and healers—are the often-invisible aspects of nature, down to the microbes in the soil."

JUDITH D. SCHWARTZ author of *Cows Save the Planet*

"This book needs to get into the hands of as many women as possible. I couldn't put it down. It helped awaken a fire deep inside my being—a fire that inspires action, connection, and the creation of an epic future."

LAUREN FRANCES TUCKER board chair of Kiss the Ground
and director of product development for White Buffalo Land Trust

GROUNDED

GROUNDED

A Fierce, Feminine Guide to
Connecting with the Soil
and Healing from
the Ground
Up

Erin Yu-Juin McMorrow, PhD

sounds true
BOULDER, COLORADO

Sounds True
Boulder, CO 80306

Published 2021

Cover design by Jennifer Miles
Book design by Karen Polaski

The wood used to produce this book is from
Forest Stewardship Council (FSC) certified forests,
recycled materials, or controlled wood.

Printed in the United States of America

Library of Congress Cataloging-in-Publication Data
Names: McMorrow, Erin, author.
Title: Grounded : a fierce, feminine guide to connecting with the
    soil and healing from the ground up / [Erin McMorrow].
Description: Boulder, CO : Sounds True, 2021. |
    Includes bibliographical references.
Identifiers: LCCN 2020017838 | ISBN 9781683646129
    (hardcover) | ISBN 9781683646136 (ebook)
Subjects: LCSH: Soils and climate. | Soils—Carbon
    content. | Soil fertility.
Classification: LCC S596.3 .M36 2021 | DDC 631.4—dc23
LC record available at https://lccn.loc.gov/2020017838

10 9 8 7 6 5 4 3 2 1

To all the seekers, the healers, and the
stewards of the land. May our voices
come together to elevate the conversation.

Let the beauty we love be
what we do.
There are hundreds
of ways to kneel and
kiss the ground.[1]

RUMI

CONTENTS

Introduction . . . 1

PART ONE
BRASS TACKS

1   Imagine the Year 2050 . . . 17
2   The Legacy Load . . . 23
3   The Story of All Things . . . 31

PART TWO
THE CRY OF ALL WOMEN

4   How Did We Get Here? . . . 49
5   The Cry of All Women . . . 59

PART THREE
HEALING FROM THE GROUND UP

6   Inner Work and Outer Work Are One . . . 81
7   Returning to Our Roots . . . 93
8   We Are Inherently Worthy . . . 101
9   Remembering We Are Nature:
    Growing Our Own Food . . . 107
10 Facing Death and Regeneration: Compost and
    Healing with Indigenous Peoples and Lands . . . 117

PART FOUR
INTEGRATION: DIVINE
FEMININE AND DIVINE MASCULINE

11 Living a Regenerative Life . . . 127
12 Owning Our Power . . . 141
13 What's Possible . . . 155
14 The Divine Dance . . . 163

Acknowledgments . . . 169
Notes . . . 173
About the Author . . . 179

Are you afraid
Of the void?

The fertile soil
The fertile soul
Where seeds come to life

Crack open
Fight for light

In darkness we grow
From the void we emerge

New moon
Bloody flow

Where'd she go

Welcome to
The collective blind spot

The collective wound
Death
Release
Decomposition
Rebirth

She is the garden
There is no exile

She simply holds space
For us to finally face

The eternal truth

How could this be
What can't we see

Cycles unbroken
Simply imbalanced
Return again and again

Connect the dots
My lovers and friends

The wound only heals
When we face in

The humble worm
8-legged goddess
Infinity creatrix
Night sky
Everlasting

There's only one way home
Turn in
Tune in

Yin yang
Up down
In out

Breath reveals
Holy love heals

Follow the drumbeat
Look toward the light
Bow to the night

The portal
The vortex
The mother

The spiral
The beat

The virgin
Woman unto herself

Sexual healing
That's what I said

As above so below
What are we pretending we don't know

Welcome the muse
Of creation and transformation
Priestesses
Of transmutation
Goddesses
Of liberation

Bow to the great mother
Remember
The soil
Stuff of stars

The humble answer
Rebirthing the only truth
There ever was

INTRODUCTION

Take three breaths. Allow the skin of the old to shed away and welcome the possibility of what's to come. We are rebirthing ourselves and midwifing a new era, a new world, a new vision. Walk with me into a world of possibility, alignment, love, and truth.

The root of the climate crisis is the invitation to heal our individual and collective root chakra (as it was first known in the Hindu tantric traditions, although our ancient connection to the earth is universal). Our root is our base, foundation, home, identity, innate power, release, safety, security, structure, and connection to the earth. Humanity teeters at the edge of extinction because for too long we have been too afraid to remember. To come home. To turn inward. For thousands of years, we have been handing over our power to institutions, ideas, and individuals outside of ourselves. For way too long, we've bought into the story that we can somehow derive our power from external things—social status, relationships, property, objects, titles, degrees, even talents and knowledge. We've believed that nature herself is dangerous, our enemy, and that she is meant to be tamed, mined, and owned. We've bowed to a single male god in the sky and lashed out at the notion of an embodied spiritual truth that incorporates the balance of the sacred feminine and sacred masculine in the grand harmony of all things within us.

The feminine and masculine energies are not specific to gender; they are part of each of us. We are working with the dance between steady structure and fluid receiving energy; the calm protector and initiator of the masculine, and the flowing, adaptable, womb-like creative nature of the feminine. As we find balance within ourselves, we become better able to create balance in our outer worlds. Reconnecting with our lower chakras also reconnects us to our roots, the story of the earth, the Great Mother, and our own creative life force energy. We remember that we are part of the grand dance of all things.

Climate catastrophe, biodiversity loss, the sixth mass extinction, ocean acidification, desertification, and runoff and dead zones in the oceans are all connected to the same thing: the killing of microscopic life in the soil. Our disconnection from the soil is our disconnection from the fertile feminine. By killing this life en masse, we are profoundly disrupting the carbon cycle, along with all the cycles of nature. While the entire movement of regenerative agriculture (a form of agriculture that focuses on improving soil health) has made significant headway with this message in the climate conversation, the memo has yet to go mainstream. Most of us have never heard of soil's critical connection to the climate emergency. Even fewer of us are aware of the profound spiritual connections among the earth, climate, and the interrelatedness of all things. Understanding ourselves as a part of nature—as opposed to as separate entities who affect nature—is fundamental to this larger view.

Further, the connection between empowering women and girls and turning the tide on the climate emergency is clear. Access to education and reproductive rights are at the heart of the dire situation we have collectively created. Katharine Wilkinson of Project Drawdown highlights the role of women in food production on small lots, describing how that work ties in with protection of forests, as well as how reproductive education and rights have as much (or more) of an impact on our collective climate footprint as renewable energy.[1] Wilkinson urges us to be messengers, hearts broken open, in this journey. Protecting our forests, getting into right relationship with animals, plants, and fungi, healing our food systems, and freeing and protecting women and girls from poverty, genital mutilation, sexual assault and harassment, and sex trafficking, are all mission critical to creating human systems aligned with Mother Nature.

The only way to return to balance is to heal the Earth Mother and our collective root chakra—as well as our own individual roots—and to harmonize the feminine and masculine energies within ourselves. This also means simultaneously working to heal the soil, supporting indigenous peoples and lands, and advocating for women and girls around the world. As above, so below; the macro reflects the micro, and vice versa.

You may already know that soil is one of the most important things in the world when it comes to human survival, right up there with water and oxygen. But likely you have little idea of what that means on a practical level, or what to do about it. It's actually incredibly simple, and we already have everything we need to shift our systems on earth. All we need is to remember, align, and act. As we heal our connection to the soil, we move toward healing our bodies, the earth, and our spirits.

Life is a miracle. Microscopic processes inside the cells of plants convert sunlight into energy that we humans, in turn, can use. Not only use, but *need* for survival. Pause there for a moment. Take a breath . . . wow. The only way to understand the world of the small things that make all life on earth possible is to trace back to the first life, our friends the single-celled organisms. Microscopic life was the first on earth, and nobody knows for sure how it came to be. Our best guesses involve comets or curious vibrations in the primordial soup (so, basically, magic, god, aliens, or . . . something).

The divine mysteries (Spirit), life on earth (body), and our evolutionary history (science) have everything to do with soil health and climate change. It's all connected, and the only way to solve the problem is to take it all in, magic included. I'm not talking about the kind of delusional magical thinking we've been engaged in as a species thus far; I'm talking about real magic. Mysteries of life and creativity magic. If we follow the thread from the primordial soup and through our basic cellular evolution, we can make our way to the present-day carbon cycle and everything that's wrong with it. We can do better by healing the soil, healing ourselves, and healing our relationship with the Great Mother and all that is.

The soil is alive. All of nature is connected. And we are profoundly connected to the soil and each other. Carbon is the building block of life. If we manage to figure this out and act on it in short order, we can avoid running ourselves into extinction. Healing the soil by repairing the microscopic life we've been killing, healing with indigenous peoples and lands, and uplifting women and girls are the most important things we can do to repair vital earth systems right now. This is healing the sacred. And the feminine. The good news is, if you have the luxury to read this, you are someone who can do something about it.

Tuning in to the cycles of nature and becoming aware of what makes both the earth and our bodies tick can help us understand what life is all about. Sustainability is about the sacred connections with all of life. We are souls having a human experience. We are embodied. And we are physically made of the same stuff as everything else. We are in some form of symbiosis with everything that lives and in direct symbiosis with soil life, which we have been killing for some time now with our ignorance, unconsciousness, and disconnectedness. By killing life in the soil, we are essentially killing ourselves. And it will take reconnecting and recultivating life where it is currently being harmed—underground—to right the balance. By reconnecting and healing the soil, we honor the life within us all. From dead zones in the ocean, to clean drinking water, to the amount of nutrients in the very food we eat, to how we care for ourselves and each other, this is the story of everything.

Crossing the threshold we currently face will require the courage to turn inward into the darkness, into the lies, and into the shadowy untruths that have defined humanity for thousands of years. It will require us to tune in to our deepest knowing, our bodies, and our own collective shadow to discover the truth—the truth that is ever present and always underfoot, the truth of the suppressed divine feminine in harmony with the suppressed divine masculine. When we choose *in*, when we choose to face the fire and go directly into our suppressed pain, we'll find freedom on the other side—as long as we support each other through the process.

Ultimately, we'll find our earthly survival and cultivate our path to thriving through Mother Nature. The Mother Goddess. Pachamama. Gaia. The fertile soil. The divine feminine. She houses the seed, life gestates in the dark, new life is born, and eventually it returns back to the Mother. We have forgotten that we belong to the land, not the other way around. We get to remember that while we are healing her, she is healing us.

I'm pointing straight at the most important Western cultural, societal, and psychological blind spot: the Great Earth Mother goddess is feminine sexuality and the sexuality of nature. She is the void, death, birth, grief, and fertility. She is the birth-giving, life-giving, magic-making creatrix. The night sky and the moon. The divine order of chaos. The lunar seed metaphor represents the cycles of nature, the harvest, the seasons, and menstruation: gestation, birth, life, death, and rebirth. She cannot be owned. We belong to the land and we belong to ourselves. The fertile, living soil is the collective blind spot. And our blindness is killing us. This book is a direct shot at opening the third eye of patriarchy.

I learned an incredibly important thing from the field of urban planning: a non-decision is a de facto decision (illustrated in excruciating clarity by the federal COVID-19 response in the United States). Outcomes will arise from either acting or not acting. And in this case, either action or inaction will have major effects. If we do not act, the amount of carbon in the atmosphere and the oceans will continue to rise, while the amount in the soils will continue to fall—to the lasting detriment of the soils, which means to ourselves.

The good news is that there is something we can actually do about it. If we choose to, we can build a world and the systems we desire with our own hands. We can get to work, do what it takes to potentially save ourselves, and create something regenerative, harmonious, and beautiful for the future.

Summoning the courage to take on this work will require that we look the problems at hand directly in the eye.

CONNECTING THE DOTS

This personal journey has been divinely guided and this book is my offering. I entered this path upside down and backwards, and have been birthed and rebirthed along the way. Originally, in an effort to wake up humanity to both the dire state of current conditions and to what might be possible, I began with the intention of laying out a scientific argument about soil health and climate change. Much to my amusement now, I had no idea what I actually signed up for. After years of spiritual journeying, I have finally landed at the feet of the Great Earth Mother, the creatrix, the dark goddess. This journey continues to guide me through the lands of the suppressed and oppressed: indigenous ways of knowing, storytelling, shamanism, feminism, witches, ceremony, divination, sacred sexuality, the oppression of women and girls, and plant medicine. I explore several of these in this book, although I focus more on the role of the soil in our climate emergency, as well as the role of inner work within individual soul recovery.

The voice of the divine feminine—the bringer of life and the overseer of death and rebirth—has guided my hand at each turn. And in each personal rebirth and soul retrieval of my own, the eternal message remains the same: everything is interconnected. The universe is alive, benevolent, and co-creative, and nature is always speaking to us, as we are part of her.

My job in this moment, as part of the collective ecosystem, is to firmly and boldly anchor the truth wherever I stand. Humanity is moving through a metamorphic awakening of consciousness, and teams of light-bearers are assembling to help guide the process. As we pass into this collective rebirth, we also move through a collective death. Patriarchal systems and ways of being are crumbling and collapsing all around us, and what has been built atop centuries of lies can no longer stand. Without the structural integrity of a healthy root system, our castles are built on sand. The resonant voice of nature herself—and all of us as a part of her—is rising up in love. And the force is unstoppable. Consciousness itself is being reborn as the universe continues to align, breathe, recognize, and make love with itself.

The rebalancing of the sacred feminine and sacred masculine energies is inevitable. And it's happening all around us, as the natural alignment of the universe brings humans into balance with the greater whole. This book is a guidebook, a lighthouse, and a flag post to help you navigate and orient yourself in the changing tides. I specifically intend to simplify the complex and help connect the dots among the soil, the climate, the divine feminine, the goddess, and the healing of women and girls on this earth. The way forward requires our own personal work, meeting that inner work with outer work in the world, and understanding that all of this is interdependently connected.

We can't truly connect with ourselves without understanding how we're connected with each other and everything around us—physically with our breath, the food we eat, and the constant turnover of our cells. And we are all energetically connected through the great web of life, death, and rebirth. We've always known this as humans; we've merely forgotten. This book is about remembering who we are. Remembering we are one. With each other, with the earth, and with the divine. This truth has been rewritten, co-opted, obscured, and cast aside. Navigating our way back actually requires us to face our fears directly and integrate them, and to approach those fears as exiled parts of ourselves. We are infinitely, intimately interconnected. Inherently in balance with all there is and all there ever was.

> What we call the beginning is often the end.
> And to make an end is to make a beginning.
> The end is where we start from.[2]
>
> T. S. ELIOT

MY JOURNEY

Before we get into the brass tacks, I want to share some of my personal journey with you. I'm not here to tell you how it is. I'm a messenger, and I'm here to share what I've discovered. When I embarked upon this journey years ago, I had no idea that the soil is the oldest divine feminine metaphor of all time. Neither did I know much about life in the soil and, in fact, I probably knew zero about its relationship to climate change. Even with a PhD in Urban Planning.

My process has been an unveiling and unraveling, as well as a sincere surrender. When we say yes to Spirit, we often end up drinking from the fire hose of new information and associations, in my case for more than seven years, which is both an eternity and the blink of an eye. Everything about this was considered wacky when I started. Over these years, the wheel has been turning, and peers in the regenerative agriculture movement have brought the story of the soil from relative obscurity to front and center in the climate conversation. Simultaneously, colleagues have been recovering, piecing together, and sharing ancient wisdom about goddess history, the divine feminine and masculine, and plant medicine, and have offered the healing experiential aspect of this story far more deeply into the mainstream. When I began this journey, these worlds were seemingly disparate and incompatible. I struggled profoundly with society's insistence that I fit in a box somewhere recognizable to others. Spiritual growth is bumpy, beautiful, confronting, hilarious, and always humbling. Coming out of the woo closet has been my most challenging obstacle and my greatest opportunity. The bumps and triumphs in my path have been many.

My first face plant came in 2013 (heading toward what I now recognize as a classic spiritual breakdown), right after I graduated with my doctorate. I really thought I had my life figured out at the time. I had been writing like a madwoman for months, with a ferocity that I've only recently matched since. I completed my dissertation, defended it, and celebrated. My family flew in from all over, my dad opened the good wine, and we had a rager. Utterly exhausted, I dropped off my last guest (my mom) at LAX and then came home to find out that the awesome house I'd been leasing was going up for sale. To top it off, I'd almost spent what was left of my dissertation fellowship.

There it went: six years of structure and purpose, all of my income, and my house. I had no plan whatsoever. Fortunately, I'm a seasoned budget traveler and a little bit of a hustler, so I was able to string together some odd jobs and rented out my own home for survival for a few months as I threw myself into the job search. I knew it would all come together—I had a PhD, for crying out loud, and there was opportunity everywhere.

A friend of mine named Chance (yes, that's his real name) said, "There's this volunteer group I think you'd love. It's about how healing soil solves all these sustainability problems, and we're building an urban garden in Venice [CA]." I can't remember specifically what he said, but what I do remember is that as he was speaking, I saw it all click into place.

I started attending the volunteer group meetings and stayed quiet. Every week, a group of us gathered in my friend Ryland's living room to discuss strategies and next steps. The group had been meeting for a few months already. The host's family had founded a wildly popular vegan restaurant in California, and so he was looped into the local organic food scene. He had heard soil consultant Graeme Sait speak at a conference in Australia, and it had propelled him on a mission to spread the word, because Graeme had been the only speaker to offer solutions (whereas the others just went on and on about the doom and gloom state of the earth).

I listened quietly at first to the discussions about compost and crowdfunding and building an urban garden. I did what I could to contribute my time and expertise while still looking for a job and moving. Those first few months were madcap: We built a garden from scratch and threw a launch party, only to have the garden promptly torn down by the landowner (who wanted to put a giant condo there). We had heated conversations about becoming an organization and raising money. Would we be a business, a B-Corp, or a nonprofit? And for god's sake what was our mission? To educate? Tell the story? Plant gardens? We storyboarded and began a crowdfunding campaign. Then we invited Graeme to town for a big party. Someone asked him the obvious question: What should we should focus on? He replied, "City-level policy. We need to get cities composting." When I brought up my policy experience and knowledge, Graeme asked, "Will you be going to the mayor's office with us?" I hadn't, until that point, been invited. Until then, I had been lying low, and suddenly found myself in the middle of the process.

We went, and it was exciting to share the story of the soil with city officials, but it was just a speck in what would eventually come to be. From there we thrashed onward, fueled by passion and rowdy idealism. I became the first director of the group and threw everything I had into it. I was already used to not making a lot of money, and my primary focus was getting my hands on something aimed at making a significant difference. I spent countless hours on the phone and at our meetings, trying to chart a course for a group of volunteers to transform us into a functional, funded organization.

We had absolutely no idea what we were doing, but I've never seen such a committed group of people. They donated untold hours of their lives for a cause, driven by the genuine belief that our broken relationship with soil is the problem, the story, and the call to action of our generation. After an enormously long and ridiculous search for identity, we secured a seed grant and a lawyer, and started down the road to becoming a 501(c)(3) nonprofit organization we named Kiss the Ground. We began work on *The Soil Story*—an animated film that describes soil's relationship to climate, humans, and the ecosystem at large.

At that point, I had to take a break. I had been cracking for a while—barely scraping by and forced to move yet again. The startup process of building something out of nothing had been extremely hard on my heart, too, and I felt ravaged after the jolts of graduation, two displacements, and a variety of other losses along the way. By 2014, it was time for a change. I decided to put all my stuff into storage, fly to Indonesia for yoga teacher training, slow down, and get some clarity. I knew that my whole soul was called to work on this issue, but I was no longer meant to be in the center of Kiss the Ground. I had imagined that the well-paying post-PhD dream job that I was certain to acquire would have arrived by then, and it hadn't. I had suppressed my desire to pursue yoga teacher training, because until that point it felt like anything other than chasing after my dream job was irresponsible.

As I was pondering my next move, a childhood friend suddenly passed away of a fast-moving cancer. She was my age with two small children and a husband. I realized that I'd regret not going to Bali if it were me finding out I was going to die. It was a giant leap that went against everything I was raised to believe was a good, responsible decision. Interestingly enough, this book started to come through me on the plane to Bali.

The experience was utterly transformative and easily one of the best decisions I've ever made. I entered the worlds of personal and spiritual healing modalities, working with subtle energies and the mind-body-spirit connection. It's here that I came to learn about the chakras, found my feet, and began to shed the layers of false societal conditioning around my inner power and worthiness as a spiritual being. I picked up the scent of my wildness—my connection to nature—and started to follow it with increasing trust. I committed my life to the shift and began teaching yoga and doing healing work, as well as writing my book and building my business when I returned.

I reunited with the Kiss the Ground crew in Paris at the COP21 climate talks in December 2015, after working on this book for about a year and a half. We were together to see the words *The Soil Story* go up in lights on the Eiffel Tower. After all of the intense growing pains and stumbles we had experienced in our parallel journeys, driven by the same fire, it was profoundly healing for me (and the rest of the crew, I think). The organization was blossoming, and the regenerative agriculture movement was growing. Paris, all told, was a life-changing experience, and a heartwarming success for us soil people, especially when the French agricultural minister proposed a program called "4 per 1000" (despite it not making mainstream news). The initiative calls for countries to increase carbon in soils by 0.4 percent, which, if done worldwide, could halt the annual increase in CO_2 in the atmosphere.[3] Dozens of countries and organizations signed on. Stop for a moment and imagine the possibility.

At the same time, I was becoming a writer, an artist, and an activist. I wrote and published a 400-word version of this story with Upworthy, which had tens of thousands of likes and views in the first week. The article was even promoted by Michael Pollan—a sizable victory for me at that juncture in my career.

I met more soil allies on the ground: community group members, authors, researchers, and activists who had crossed the planet to fight for healthy soil. I learned more about how hard indigenous groups (some of the most violated people around the world) were fighting on their home turf against climate change and its causes. I would be told for the next five years that "climate change doesn't sell" with regard to books and articles, but a foundation had been laid in my spirit, and inevitably the cultural zeitgeist would shift back toward climate awareness and action. The spiritual and the practical were indeed weaving within the collective and me, but the impact of it all would only become clear in retrospect.

I also had the honor of attending the Pathway to Paris concert, where Thom Yorke's voice blew a hole in my heart and inspired a resonance that will be with me forever (he sang "Silent Spring," among other songs). Patti Smith was there, too, and her cover of Lennon's "Imagine" absolutely destroyed my friend and me, leaving us weeping in a puddle. (Side note: John Lennon had been assassinated the night I was born thiry-five years prior that same week in December, and all the artists at the concert thanked him for being in the room that night). They themselves had chosen to be there (along with Bill McKibben, Naomi Klein, and Vandana Shiva) because all of them understand that this work is about nothing less than the integrity of humanity. It's about the people who will be on this planet for the next thirty years and thereafter.

I had no idea how early in the process I still was at that time. Since then, I've experienced some of the most unexpected, difficult, fruitful, and necessary challenges yet. I bartended my way through two years of writing and creating a soul-driven business committed to individual and collective healing. I have forged my way through breakups, rejections, the concern of my family, and all manner of setbacks. Writer Linda Sivertsen says, "Trust your delays."[4] Necessary, but not easy. At first, while I was feeling like a female Chinese-Irish Don Quixote, I would reach back to that Paris trip (especially that concert) to remind myself how real and critically important this work is. By 2017 I was starting to learn how to co-create with Spirit, and I discovered that perceived setbacks are always redirections, always gifts. By this point, my faith does not falter.

As I brought this part of the project to a close, I remembered that the end is always the beginning. Which brings me to the Zen Buddhist concept called *shoshin*, or "beginner's mind." Actually, the *shin* part of the word means "heart," although unlike in Western thought, many Eastern traditions don't think of the heart and mind as two distinct entities. To enter something with the beginner's mind is to be open and willing to learn, despite what one may already know or think they know on a subject. This means letting go of judgment and criticism in order to be able to take in the new. I invite you to take on a beginner's mind as we journey into the underground world of soil microbes, and I thank you in advance for your curiosity and open-mindedness.

THE PATH

This path is simple, true, beautiful, and not for the faint of heart. Each of our souls incarnated on this planet at this particular time to play some part of this grand awakening and transformation. And not a moment too late. As Marianne Williamson says, "It may be the 11th hour, but it is not yet midnight."[5] You are holding the truth in your hands. This book is a roadmap to the new world, a simple history of what's been, and a description of what steps to take next.

Place your bare feet on the earth. Take three breaths. Follow the drumbeat of your heart. Fall forward and allow the universe to catch you. Love is our teacher, our guide, our lighthouse. May our paths inward and back toward each other be courageous and blessed. May our shadow be loved, integrated, healed, and met with humility and compassion. May we be the ones who rebirth humanity into its next, more peaceful and abundant evolution, together.

PART ONE

BRASS TACKS

Nobody said it would be easy.
We have serious work to do, and a lot
of it. To begin, we must focus on the
basics. In order to create the future
we want, we must first find our feet.

1

IMAGINE THE
YEAR 2050

I magine you're a thirty-year-old mom. It's 2020, and you have just given birth to a newborn baby. Now imagine thirty years have passed. You are sixty years old and your baby is now a thirty-year-old adult.

In 2050, the earth's population has risen to over 9.5 billion people. The oceans, as projected by NOAA scientists way back in 2014, are 70 percent more corrosive than they were, but even at that time they were already dissolving the shells of small animals.[1, 2, 3] Climate change, as projected by the Intergovernmental Panel on Climate Change (IPCC) scientists in 2013, is now completely irreversible by humans (except by a freak technology or act of god), and is pushing average temperatures well above the 2 degrees Celsius increase scientists have warned would be catastrophic.[4] More than a quarter of land species are threatened with extinction.[5] Fifty to seven hundred million people have been forced to migrate because of land turning to desert all over the world.[6] Supplies of clean drinking water and healthy soil for food are rapidly deteriorating. Half of the earth's oxygen is at risk because of threats to microscopic life in the oceans.[7] This is what it's like in 2050. Take a deep breath. And imagine.

I learned about global warming sometime in middle school. And at the time, we were taught that our grandchildren's grandchildren would have to face the problem. I remember wondering what it would be like to be part of the generation of people who would slowly come into awareness that they were it, that the future of humanity would turn on what they decided to do. I wondered how long it would take them to figure it out. Would it come slowly and creep up on them? Would they argue about it? Would people deny it? Would it fix itself before they ever got there? And how exciting it would be. And terrifying. What might it be like to be part of the most important group of people in the history of the human species? The only group to have to—and get to—consciously choose whether to survive or to perish.

IT'S TIME

It's time. Everything happened a lot more quickly than scientists back then expected it to, and it's accelerating to this day. If you expect to be alive any time in the next thirty years or beyond, you're it. There's no other group of people to pass this on to. We've kicked the can as far as it will go. If we want to create a world that we can keep living in, it's time, and it's us. It's time for us to see things as they are and to stop making excuses, and it's time to summon the courage to do the work that we all know we need to do. We have a shot, but the window is small and closing rapidly.

I know it's terrifying. But if we turn that response on its head, it's also unbelievably exciting. Everything we'll do in the next ten years is of lasting consequence. No group of humans has ever had such a collective responsibility, or such a collective opportunity. As I heard it said at the Paris climate talks in 2015, we need seven billion pairs of hands (now closer to eight billion) to do this work, to turn this ship around. It can be done, and it's going to take all of us, together.

The number one thing we need to do today, next to slowing our fossil fuel emissions to a stop, is to devote ourselves to healing soil all over the world as quickly as possible. In order to have a shot at slowing the effects of climate change, we must pull carbon out of the atmosphere. A lot of it belongs in the soil, where plants can make use of it, which is where we should store it. If you have no idea what I'm talking about, you have found the right book. For a number of reasons, this most obvious conclusion is incredibly counterintuitive for most people. In truth, it's countercultural.

My journey to this simple conclusion has not been simple in the least. But here I am, and I've already bet everything I have on it. I'm throwing down on this simple point, because it's the truth, and because it is arguably the most important thing we can know and act upon when it comes to addressing the most urgent challenges facing humankind. Here's the deal:

► There's too much carbon in the atmosphere and in the oceans for humans to fare well in the near future.

► There's a legacy load of carbon in the atmosphere, meaning that even if we were to stop all emissions 100 percent today, we would still be barreling toward a two degrees Celsius average global temperature increase and beyond. NASA calls the land and the oceans the "other half" of the carbon and climate conversation.[8]

► Soil sequesters carbon. In fact, it's a natural carbon sink. It already holds more than the atmosphere, plants, and animals combined.[9] Carbon-rich soil is good for plants and humans.

What we need is to get down to the brass tacks. In other words, we need to get back to our roots. We need to understand at the most basic level where our food comes from and how a healthy food system actually works. We must come to terms with where we are getting our water and how the water cycle actually works. And we have to ask ourselves what we're going to do with the excess carbon in the atmosphere and in the oceans and deal with how the carbon cycle actually works. How are our physical bodies connected to both the earth itself and global systems at the macro and micro levels? And how in the world do we manage our physical reality in a sane way that preserves survival and can allow for true regenerative abundance?

These are the most important questions facing humanity today, and we need a clear-eyed look at how it all works in order to figure out what to do about it. We need, more than anything, to build from the ground up and get the basics right. But first, we may very well need to take a giant step back to gain some much-needed perspective. To get clear on the basics even, it may serve us to zoom way out, and then back in.

> Only by standing in our own ground
> can we determine our future.[10]
> ANODEA JUDITH

As big as the earth may seem to us, we are in fact a whole bunch of infinitesimally small people on a tiny, finite planet. Happily, we have co-evolved with other life-forms on this planet (plant, animal, and otherwise, including the microscopic life in the soil and the oceans) to live in both symbiosis and homeostasis. In other words, in partnership and balance with all the other life-forms here.

Unfortunately, we have unwittingly disrupted critical systems, in particular the carbon and the water cycles, altering them so dramatically that it's destroying our own habitat. Because earth systems are so profoundly interconnected, we're looking at far more than rapid temperature change, sea level rise, and storms. As a result of ocean acidification, biodiversity loss, and desertification, we are currently facing the sixth mass extinction of species on the planet.[11] And our soil, that six-inch layer of life from which all of our food comes, is turning to dust all over the world. At the same time, the human population is growing exponentially. Adding two billion people to the current population over the next thirty years is the best guess, but it could be more.

The coming storms, heat waves, droughts, cities under water, and refugees are only part of the problem. We are facing threats to our food supply, our drinking water, and even our oxygen. We've lost 40 percent of our phytoplankton since 1950; phytoplankton are the bottom of the ocean's food chain and are responsible for nearly half of the world's oxygen.[12]

In 2013, CO_2 in the atmosphere reached 400 parts per million (ppm) for the first time in recorded human history;[13] in March of 2016, the average global surface temperature crossed the two degrees Celsius increase threshold beyond which scientists warn of devastation for the first time in human history—a threshold we're projected to cross for good by 2036.[14] This is all happening in real time, right now. By the time you read this, most or all of this data will be outdated, because we are moving along timelines with exponential curves. That means that nothing in our past experience is comparable to what's happening now, not to mention what's about to happen in the next thirty years and beyond.

Human survival is at stake. Without question. Everyone alive today is part of the deciding generation. Take a moment to look at what's going on in the news right now and see what is actually going on in the world. American politics (at the time of writing during the COVID-19 crisis) are in free fall. It's time to put our big-kid pants on, and, as Carl Sagan says, "make our stand." Welcome to the most critical set of decisions and actions humankind has ever had to make.

With more than half of the world's population in cities, urban sustainability and global sustainability are one and the same. The world's major population centers are growing to sizes and scales never before seen, driven by industrialization and population growth. And the key questions to figuring out how to reimagine these cities, which are currently creaking under their own weight and bursting at every seam, have everything to do with the basic needs of humans. Everything boils down to land, water, housing, food, and basic social and economic dignity. Basic needs are simple; the related problems and solutions are complex.

As cringe-worthy as the word *sustainability* has become, it has a functional and useful meaning. Ultimately, a sustainable system is one that can keep itself balanced in perpetuity, rather than being poised for collapse. A sustainable city is one that is built from such systems and is connected to larger systems that can hold their own. It's also a city where people can meet their basic needs of food, water, and shelter on a daily basis. The notion of a regenerative world takes this one step further. A regenerative world is not merely avoiding collapse, but is designed, like nature, to be abundant beyond our basic needs. A regenerative system includes replenishing what we take and inviting nature to blossom in her diversity, resiliency, and fertility.

The task at hand is to connect the individual to the collective in a healthy way. At a global scale, we need to look directly at the basics and create a plan of action. And we need to start doing it before we have all the information. If we wait until all the data about what's to come fall into place before we act, it will be way, way too late. We currently have more than enough information to act in a strategic manner and in an intelligent direction, and we can adjust and refine along the way.

This *intelligent direction* is toward healthy soil and gender equity all over the world. There are only wildly positive effects to healing soil and supporting women and girls, and we need to do these now in order to turn the climate emergency around, no matter what else we do. Unequivocally. It's a no-brainer.

2

THE LEGACY LOAD

The carbon cycle is currently out of whack as it relates to humans and most creatures on the earth. I mentioned the first big problem in the last chapter: the legacy load. We know that there's entirely too much carbon in the atmosphere and that we've long since blown past the "safe level" of 350 ppm. We crossed 400 ppm of carbon in the atmosphere on May 9, 2013, and we're still climbing.[1] According to the IPCC, it would take almost 100 years to get back to 350 ppm even if we had stopped emitting altogether in 2007.[2]

Stopping emissions is not going to be enough. Slowing emissions is definitely not going to be enough. We have to turn this ship completely around, and there's no time to half-ass it. This unpleasant information is elegantly captured in the IPCC's Fifth Assessment Report (AR5):

> Most aspects of climate change will persist
> for many centuries even if emissions
> of CO_2 are stopped. This represents a
> substantial multi-century climate change

commitment created by past, present, and
future emissions of CO_2. A large fraction
of anthropogenic climate change resulting
from CO_2 emissions is irreversible on a
multi-century to millennial time scale, except
in the case of a large net removal of CO_2 from
the atmosphere over a sustained period.[3]

Translation: To get back to where we were before, we actually
need net negative emissions. Net. Negative. We need to not only
slow and stop emissions, but to draw carbon out of the air and
store it in the earth. A lot of it, over a long time. In other words,
we need to do all the things. All. The. Things.

We're not supposed to talk about this because it will freak
people out. Either that or they'll just dismiss the data outright.
It's a lot to digest. And given how terribly we've done with the
information we already have about the need to reduce emissions,
the concern is that people will simply shut down and do nothing (or, in fact, continue to make the situation worse). We don't
have time to be stuck in fear. Even if we're afraid, we need to
lean in to it and keep moving forward, and the only way we're
actually going to be able to grapple with the problem is to get a
handle on it and face it.

I checked in with the lead author of this particular section
of the IPCC report, and he was actually hopeful that if we can
lower emissions quickly enough, we can adapt to what's currently occurring on the planet. I hope he's right. That said, if we
were to simultaneously lower emissions and move to rapidly
draw down and store carbon in the soil, it would still be of
tremendous benefit to our overall situation, no matter our level
of success in lowering emissions. In *Drawdown*, Paul Hawken
and Katharine Wilkinson do a wonderful job of covering what it
will take to heal the soil and sequester carbon in a wide variety
of ways.

In worst-case scenarios, we'd at least give ourselves a little bit more time to change our systems enough to lower emissions in the face of a growing population. In more optimistic scenarios, we actually get our act together and get ourselves on a path to net negative. Whatever happens, the earth needs to take in one large, sustained inhale. The inhale, as it happens, is the yin part of the breath. Surrendering, receiving, taking in before and after releasing. Every natural cycle, including our breath, follows this rhythm.

OCEAN ACIDIFICATION

Next to the legacy load, we face ocean acidification. The effects of the oceans absorbing more carbon than they can hold are clear. Too much carbon in the oceans causes the ocean pH to change, and our oceans are currently quickly acidifying; they are literally becoming corrosive. And excuse my French, but it's fucking terrifying. Ocean acidification is coming at us faster and more definitively than climate change, and climate change is coming at us like the proverbial freight train.

It's worth repeating: our corrosive waters are dissolving the shells of baby animals right now. At the rate we are going, waters will be 70 percent more corrosive by 2050, and the amount of sea life with dissolving shells could triple.[4] That's just twenty-nine years from the publication of this book, and counting. Perturbing the oceans is an altogether horrible idea. When researching this topic, I found utterly terrifying lines like this buried in academic papers:

> By process of elimination, primary causes
> of mass extinctions are linked in various
> ways to the carbon cycle in general, and
> ocean chemistry in particular, with clear
> association with atmospheric carbon dioxide
> levels. The prospect of ocean acidification

is potentially the most serious of all
predicted outcomes of anthropogenic carbon
dioxide increase. This study concludes
that acidification has the potential to
trigger a sixth mass extinction event and
to do so independently of anthropogenic
extinctions that are currently taking place.[5]

In case you spaced out for a moment, I recommend you go back and read this section from the top. And then take a few deep breaths. We all know that not doing anything will almost definitely result in dire consequences, and for most of us that freaks us out a great deal. Reading about the certainty of massive disasters definitely freaks me out. When I was up in a cabin doing the first round of research on all these topics, I literally had to stop—the information was so overwhelming, it was more than I could take (and I had already been studying it for six years). It makes sense that this type of news shuts us down, and we would much rather drink a beer and watch TV than deal with it or look it squarely in the face. Our conditioned response to escapism when we feel fear is not uncommon. I get it. Sometimes I'm there.

HOW DO WE TAKE ON A PROBLEM THIS BIG AND MESSY?

For my dissertation, I proposed the question, "Do sustainability plans in cities affect outcomes?" I was told that I couldn't ask that question because sustainability is hard to define, sustainability plans are multifaceted, and cities are nearly impossible to quantify (an endless problem for urban planning academics). The odds of finding a defensible answer were low with all these messy variables, and in choosing a question, I was reminded, we need to select something that we can measure. We generally punt the big, weird, or unmeasurable questions.

My advisors were being kind and doing their jobs, of course, as they didn't want me to step into an impossible intellectual morass and never graduate. But luckily, my primary advisor asked, "If we don't ask the big, messy questions, who will?" So I was permitted to carry on, and eventually I defended my dissertation, drawing on existing quantitative data, qualitative interview techniques, storytelling, critical thinking, and creative problem solving.

Nature—which includes the earth, the universe, and all of us—is big and almost endlessly complex. Its complexity is partly why the notion of environmental sustainability is so hard to nail down, define, and fully comprehend. One field that is actually quite good at thinking about and understanding systems, naturally, is the field of ecology. Unfortunately, in the world of experts, we have also overdeveloped our specialization muscles, and so people in different fields have a tough time talking to each other. Even people in related subfields are not the best at understanding each other's research. So, for example, microbiologists, marine biologists, agricultural soil scientists, and climate scientists are mostly not attending the same conferences nor reading one another's papers, and generally are not communicating with one another at all. This stymies our problem-solving abilities and keeps us in our insular silos, often scratching our heads, missing information from other fields that could be useful.

Personally, one fun aspect of this whole journey is that in relearning the basics of things like photosynthesis, the divine and the practical have finally started to come together for me. Once again, I've learned that in order to expand out, I have to go in. The things we haven't dealt with inside manifest on the outside. When it comes to the earth and the carbon cycle, one broken part of the system is the soil—to get it, we have to look inside and unpack it. The first thing to know, in the simplest terms, is that the carbon cycle roughly includes the atmosphere, the oceans, and the soil (including the smaller category of vegetation). It's like the water cycle, in the sense that it's finite and carbon changes forms throughout the cycle. Most of us learned this in school at some point and either vaguely remember or totally forgot about it.

We hear that carbon is the building block of life, but most of us have no idea what that means. Our lack of understanding is actually not terribly surprising, as carbon is almost incomprehensibly small. Not stuff most of us think about every day. Carbon is one of the most basic and mundane things around, and also one of the most miraculous—the stuff of charcoal was originally born from stars. And it cruises around the earth, atmosphere, and oceans, going wherever it is sent.

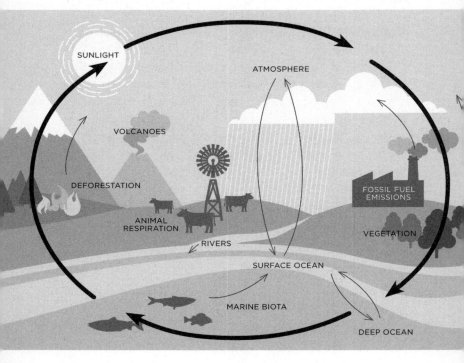

Carbon Cycle

Right now there is far too much carbon in the atmosphere and oceans, and not enough at all in the soil. The oceans absorb the carbon spillover from the atmosphere, which has been beneficial for a while, but by now the oceans are over-saturated. This is not good at all, because as we now know, all that extra carbon is making our oceans more acidic. That's terrifying, and again, nearly incomprehensible in terms of what the negative consequences could be for humanity. One more time: ocean acidification is at least as big of a problem as climate change, although few are talking about it in the mainstream. Clearly, to bring the carbon cycle back into balance, we urgently need to bring carbon out of the atmosphere and put it somewhere. And as the oceans and atmosphere are swamped, the place for the carbon to go is back into the soil.

3

THE STORY OF
ALL THINGS

We are carbon-based life-forms, and are therefore part of the carbon cycle. As such, we are connected to all other parts of the cycle: the oceans, the atmosphere, plant life, and the soil. The element carbon moves through these parts in a sort of endless loop, each aspect intricately interconnected with the others. At every point, there are tiny life-forms, microorganisms (or microbes) that help the cycle along. These beings matter a great deal; they need our help, and we need theirs.

They live in the oceans, they live in our bodies (mostly in our guts), and they live in the soils. We ourselves are made up of at least half microbe cells.[1] So, in a real sense, we are at least half microbe. Which makes sense, because microscopic life was the first life on this planet, from which all the rest evolved, and it currently represents the vast majority of all life on earth.[2] There is no "us" without microbes. Again, this is not something most of us are exactly thinking about on a standard Sunday afternoon, but doing so offers a serious shift in perspective around exactly who we are and what life on earth is all about.

We not only evolved from these creatures, but we are in constant symbiosis with them, day in and day out. They help us with digestion and just about everything else our bodies do. Every single cell in our bodies is in relationship with microscopic life, and as if that weren't enough, these littles also help plants to grow, they produce oxygen in the oceans, and, amazingly, they help store carbon in the soil. We are life partners, functioning side by side with these little buggers in just about every way, and we have been engaged in this funny, miraculous dance with them for as long as we have existed (although they existed long before we were even a twinkle in the cosmic eye). It might actually serve us to consider ourselves their dependents, as we can't live without them for one moment, although they can get along okay without us. Regardless, our relationship to these creatures defines our existence on this planet.

But it doesn't stop there. Within every cell in our bodies, as well as the cells of every animal on the planet, live something called mitochondria—the mission-critical part of the cell that produces energy. This little organelle is most likely the ancestor of ancient bacteria. It carries a separate bacteria-like DNA, so while we need it to work for us to be human, it is decidedly not human. And in every plant cell, the energy-producing (in this case photosynthesizing) organelle is called a chloroplast. This thing also carries its own DNA and is most likely the direct ancestor of cyanobacteria, one of the first life-forms on earth and the one probably responsible for inventing photosynthesis and literally making all other life on earth possible.[3] Every living cell then, both plant and animal, is in direct relationship to the original microscopic life that made all other life possible. We are ancestors, co-creators, and life partners with bacteria.

We also can't live for a moment without the microscopic life that lives in the soil. The words *human* and *humility* actually derive from the Latin word *humus* and the Greek *hamai*, which both mean "earth" or "ground." Sadly, in spite of our profound relationship with these tiny beings, we seem to be entirely

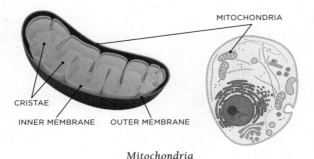

Mitochondria

unaware of their existence, not just in our bodies but also in the soil (as well as the oceans).

We've only started to truly understand what's been going on down in the soil since the 1980s, which is remarkable, considering how important the soil is to our entire existence. While we are doing our funny dance with microbes, all the plants in the world are also doing theirs. Microbes and minerals in the soil, in partnership with sunlight and water, are the champions that make energy and nutrients (read: food) available to our bodies, among many other miraculous things. In forgetting about these tiny ones, we have managed to unwittingly enact a substantial deal of damage to ourselves and to the systems of our planet.

Indeed, we have been killing this small life in the soil for quite some time, ever since we began tilling the land. By tilling the land, leaving it bare, and using pesticides on it, we've actually been wreaking havoc on the otherwise lively community below. This is unfortunate for everyone involved, as these little life-forms are responsible for bringing minerals to plant roots (which in turn bring minerals into our bodies) and cleansing and making space for water in the soil. They are also responsible for bringing carbon down through plants to be stored in the soil, forming stable, carbon-rich humus and healthy topsoil.

As it turns out, our killing of this underground community has led to the destruction of around 75 billion tons of topsoil each year by agriculture as well as the release of a huge amount of soil carbon into the atmosphere.[4] According to the IPCC, this has amounted to more than 300 billion tons of carbon moving from the soil into the atmosphere over the last 200 years.[5] This massacre also causes runoff, desertification (rich land turning to desert, think the Dust Bowl in America and Canada in the 1930s), and biodiversity loss, to name a few of the ill effects of our hapless doings.

Again, we are all connected. We must stop killing these small creatures and actually start repopulating them. Back to the brass tacks. We've managed to upend the system, and the place to start healing it is in the soil. Once we can accept that our planet is finite, we can also realize that Mother Nature is infinitely abundant if we work with her instead of against her.

The good news, of course, is that once we understand a little about life in the soil, we can help repopulate it. And, thank goodness, helping it repopulate is not terribly difficult, particularly compared to other ideas about how to get carbon back into the ground. Some are attempting to pull carbon down with machines and store it in rocks and such, but so far these technologies have proven to be prohibitively expensive and not nearly as effective as what the plants and soil can naturally do.

Not only does storing carbon in the soil help sort out the atmosphere and the oceans, it's actually good for the soil. Healthy soil is rich in carbon and microbial life, which means food full of nutrients, which in turn supports a diverse array of other life-forms in addition to purifying and storing water. For just about every reason, healing life in the soil is an overwhelmingly positive thing. And since there is no downside to healing the soil, we ought to (and need to) heal as much soil as quickly as possible in every way possible all over the world. And that means repopulating microbial life in the soil, which is relatively affordable and manageable, especially when you consider the destruction we are otherwise facing.

To get from where we are to where we want to go, we need to get crystal clear on this. Imagine looking down at your bare feet and seeing there a bunch of dark, rich, healthy soil, full of microscopic life. This is where the story begins. If you're looking for Spirit, sometimes it can help to look down.

Now, imagine microscopic life in the soil as the bottom of the food chain. Killing the bottom of the food chain eventually kills everything else above. We're not only doing harm to the place from which we come, we're destroying our partners in life—not a pretty sight for us, or for any of the other beings on this planet. So the main thing we need to do is to stop killing these little life-forms, and actually start helping them instead.

In doing their little soil dance, microbes essentially barter carbon for minerals and nutrients with plant roots. This results in healthier plants and healthier soil. Microbes are the middle-men. Voilà! When the system is working, this is what we want: nutrients up, carbon down. The soil loves carbon. It needs carbon. Imagine, in a way, that plants eat sunshine and poop carbon, and soil eats carbon. A tad oversimplified, but you get the picture. From the original primordial soup, this dance has been worked out and perfected over millennia. It's the dance of all life on Earth, imperceptible to the human eye, and absolutely mission critical.

The fact that this isn't common knowledge is frankly a little bit nuts. We unwittingly kill the stuff that makes the system work, and then spend money to replace what we've lost with synthetic replacements that don't work anywhere near as well. All the while, by disrupting the smaller system, we are of course disrupting the larger systems.

Stop and breathe it in for a moment: photosynthesis is truly mind-blowing. Magical green things called chloroplasts inside of plant cells turn the sun's radiation into chemical energy. And if that isn't wondrous enough, this process splits the carbon dioxide and water the plant has taken in, creates sugars for the plant, and releases the oxygen back into the air.

The way plants sequester carbon, weirdly, is with a combination of photosynthesis and microbes. In a magnificent exchange, the plant brings in carbon dioxide from the air and turns it into organic carbon in a form that is usable and delicious to microorganisms in the soil.[6] While some of the carbon stays in the plant body for energy, some gets bartered through the plant roots via a special fungi that partners up with the roots (called mycorrhizal fungi). This carbon stays stably stored deep in the ground in the form of humus.[7]

Silently, and without any fanfare, plants and microbes are doing more work and moving more carbon than all of humanity, day in and day out.[8] This is the miraculous, infinite dance of nature and the gift of the Great Mother. As Paul Stamets says, "[The mycelium network] is the foundation of the food web. It holds all life together. Yet these vast underground networks, which can achieve the largest masses of any organism in the world and can cover thousands of acres, hide in plain sight; silent but sentient and always working tirelessly to create the soils that sustain life."[9]

In fact, in comparison to this marvelous, perfect process, our tube-sucking-carbon-from-power-plant-pipes schemes appear rather awkward and unnecessary, if not totally absurd. There may be a role for human-made sequestration schemes, but it's worth noting that every plant is already a perfect "machine" fit to do the job. *Sequester* is a funny word. It means to hide away, to make separate, or to isolate. We humans have invested billions of dollars in human-made carbon sequestration, yet at the same time, plants are silently chugging along in the overlooked yet insanely miraculous act of photosynthesis. And when microbes are thriving in the soil and working in symbiosis with the plants, they're pulling carbon into the soil. One more time: plants pull carbon out of the atmosphere and deposit it into the soil (for free) when microscopic life thrives there. It's the way the system is already designed.

Overall, we should direct our attention to the places where soil is not already healthy. The basic way we restore life in the soil is by repopulating the microbial life that has been destroyed, which repairs the linkages and restores the natural symbiotic systems that automatically pull carbon in from the atmosphere and store it in the soil. It's not effing rocket science. In fact, it's incredibly simple.

There's a Chinese saying, *xiao bing li da gong*, which means "small soldier who does extraordinary things." Our microbial friends may be small, but they are indeed mighty.

> It is a natural human impulse to think of
> evolution as a long chain of improvements,
> of a never-ending advance towards
> largeness and complexity—in a word,
> towards us. We flatter ourselves.[10]
>
> BILL BRYSON

In honor of the small and mighty, may I introduce to you the main microbe that works with plants to pull carbon into the ground: mycorrhizal fungi, which attach to the roots of plants

Mycelium

and symbiotically work with 80 percent of them.[11] These humble mycorrhiza are perhaps the most important living organisms on earth that few people have ever heard of. They work with both the plant and the soil microbes to facilitate an ongoing exchange of nutrients and minerals, water, and carbon, as well as help to fix nitrogen in the soil.

Tragically, we've unwittingly managed to kill more than half of all mycorrhizal fungi in the world. Again, however important we may think we are, we actually live in a world determined by the very small. Matt Ridley, author of *Genome*, writes:

> The pope notwithstanding, the human species is by no means the pinnacle of evolution. Evolution has no pinnacle and there is no such thing as evolutionary progress. Natural selection is simply the process by which life-forms change to suit the myriad opportunities afforded by the physical environment and by other life-forms. The black-smoker bacterium, living in a sulphurous vent on the floor of the Atlantic Ocean and descended from a stock of bacteria that parted company with our ancestors soon after Luca's day, is arguably more highly evolved than a bank clerk, at least at the genetic level. Given that it has a shorter generation time, it has had more time to perfect its genes.[12]

If mycorrhizal fungi could talk (and use limbs), they would likely smack themselves in the foreheads and ask us what in the world is the matter with us. Never mind biting the hand that feeds us—we are literally killing the thing that possesses the hand to feed us (okay, they don't have hands, but you get the picture).

Tardigrade

As an example of the greatness of small things, check out this microscopic fellow called the water bear (technically, the tardigrade). This photo was taken with an electron microscope. Water bears are able to live in the vacuum of space, at extreme pressures, in intense heat and cold, under ionizing radiation, and without food or water for at least ten years. I introduce this fascinating creature in the hopes that you will Wikipedia them and become as obsessed as I have (and to point out just how weird and diverse life on earth really is). Just because life is tiny, doesn't mean it can't be effing cool.

To review, we are not nearly as important as we think we are, and in a bit of hubris, we are somehow managing to kill our little partners in crime below the soil line. Again, the main culprits are the ways we have exposed the soil through tilling (in addition to poor livestock management), not using compost and cover crops to replenish and protect the soil, and employing pesticides and other chemicals. The basic concept behind maintaining and supporting soil life is to replicate nature's processes as closely as possible. This means keeping the soil relatively covered and undisturbed, and relying on compost, cover crops, and other beneficial crops to protect the soil and keep it replenished with nutrients. This form of practice is referred to as regenerative agriculture.

Here's a checklist for not killing our beloved soil microbe buddies:

1   Create compost (let organic waste decompose
    rather than throwing it in the trash)
2   Use that compost instead of industrial
    fertilizers and pesticides
3   Avoid turning or tilling the soil and use cover crops
4   Amend the soil with microbes

Of course, there are different methods of composting and all sorts of details that have to do with what type of soil you are working with in the first place, but these are the relevant basics across the board. Again, not rocket science. Stu Campbell's book *Let It Rot! The Gardener's Guide to Composting* is a good starting place for step one. The best way to work with the soil wherever you are is to meet with garden shop owners; experienced gardeners; people who practice regenerative, biodynamic, and permaculture farming; and mushroom enthusiasts. This is important, because soil varies widely from region to region (even within microregions), and we have to educate ourselves instead of relying on convenient one-size-fits-all solutions. With the basics in place, the personal education and trial-and-error nature of learning to work with a specific parcel of earth is a significant part of the fun. And knowing that we're contributing to the greater good while fostering life through love and attention is its own reward.

BENEFITS OF HEALTHY SOIL

Healing the soil is already a no-brainer decision, but it also generates a number of incredible side benefits, including cleaning and storing water, increasing the nutrition in plants, restoring soil structure, counteracting runoff and desertification, and increasing biodiversity.[13] Because this is how the system originally worked, restoring life to the soil essentially puts the system back into balance, and thus heals every other related system. The carbon cycle, the water cycle, and the food web are all intimately interconnected. This should come as no surprise, once we've come to terms with the interconnectedness of all things. Mother Nature is diverse, resilient, and infinitely abundant, and working with her creates a virtuous circle of positive feedback loops. The miracle and beauty of the life-death-rebirth cycle healing begets more healing. And as we turn our intention and actions towards healing, Spirit picks us up and carries us most of the way. We must only show up to do our parts, as does every other aspect of nature.

When soil microbes are healthy and doing their thing, plants actually get everything they need to be resistant to pests, obviating much of the need for pesticides. The documentary *The Biggest Little Farm*, directed by Jon Chester, illustrates how the cycles of life and death work together in symbiosis. Thriving microbial life also works with the plant and fixes nitrogen, making commercial fertilizer unnecessary. What we have been haplessly doing instead is spraying pesticides, killing the beneficial life that helps nourish the plant, and then needing to place outside sources of nutrients into the now dead soil. A bit silly, of course, and rather expensive. The obvious alternative is, of course, to sequester carbon in the soil. Wherever there is healthy soil, this process is free and is already taking place. Gaia in her perfection. In sum, healing microbial life in the soil:

▶ Sequesters carbon from the atmosphere
▶ Ensures plants get the nutrients they need, making food more nutritious and obviating the use of pesticides and herbicides
▶ Helps the soil clean and store water, creating more clean drinking water and stopping runoff (which ends dead zones in the ocean)

- ▶ Improves soil structure, counteracting desertification
- ▶ Provides more healthy soil for increased food production with less water
- ▶ Encourages biodiversity and resiliency, meaning more species of both plants and animals can rely on the soil

There are really only positive outcomes from healing the soil, and not many excuses to do otherwise.

THE SOIL IS SEXY

My goal is to start a mainstream conversation about the incredibly sexy topic of soil health. I know. Soil health. Mmmm. Inspires a burning desire in us all, doesn't it? Earthworms and nematodes, oh my. Even better, I want to talk about not only soil health, but to link it with the irresistible topic of climate emergency. David Roberts says that talking about climate change is like passing gas at a cocktail party.[14] But if I do my job here, I will convince you that soil health is actually the sexiest thing around. This story has a way of taking hold, and once you know about it, you can't un-know it. And once you get it, you have to do something about it.

I think this confidence in the soil is the main reason the story struck me so profoundly and has stayed with me so completely. I know how potent of a power is lying in wait. When we realize that the Great Mother herself and all of fertility lies in the soil and the womb, we begin to reconnect with the eternal. When we awaken our suppressed relationship to the soil, the earth, our bodies, and our sexuality, we begin to feel the great dance and song of all life within us.

Long before this embodied awakening in me (when I was still very much in my head), the story of the soil struck me at first as something to pay attention to because of everything I already knew about global sustainability. There were a few things I knew for sure when I graduated. First, for us to perturb the oceans to the degree we currently are, things are going drastically wrong for the planet. Second, nature is a smarter designer than humans are, and we need to emulate nature in the way we make things, design cities, build houses, and deal with food and food waste. Third, we are simply not going to be able to redesign or change cities fast enough to counter the pace of climate change by improving the built environment alone. And most of us know that we need to change energy sources dramatically, as well as alter the way we live, in order to put a dent in climate change. But I've also learned other things since then.

My first soil *aha* moment (and the moment I began to tumble down the rabbit hole) actually came after I graduated, and I discovered that my training was the thing that laid the pathway to that moment. In my doctoral work, I focused almost entirely on solutions as a matter of principle and intellectual curiosity. When I bumped into the idea of soil as a solution, something clicked. And as I dug deeper (the soil puns never end in my world), all the pieces started to fall into place.

We know that dealing with the natural world the way we are now is not serving us. We're wrecking the planet. And the pervasive notion that being connected to our food (and our bodies) is somehow weak or overly emotional is tragic and dangerous.

I began the process of writing about the carbon cycle and microbes with a narrow lens, but then the wisdom of the fungal kingdom, my own body, plant medicine, Spirit, and Mother Nature herself swooped in to deliver a greater message for the highest good. Interestingly enough, at the same time I'm seeing widening circles of sisters and brothers working together to create the new economy, the new healing work, the new agriculture, the new technology, the new cities, the new relationships, the new loving, the new communicating, the new intimacy, the new dying.

We are headed into the new freedom. We are building our freedom from the inside out. Person by person, we are helping to guide and support each other along. When we realize that all things move in cycles, we no longer have to fear the darkness, the night, or death. Death brings new life, and life is eternal. Freedom is actually on the other side of our fear of death. Look to the soil. She will teach you. Look to compost; it has a message. The mundane is the awesome. The simple is the spectacular. The erotic is everything, and the dance is ongoing.

Take a breath and notice what's possible. Notice what's already available to us, every single day. And breathe into the distance between how we are currently relating to the soil and how we could otherwise be in balance. Feel into the damage we have been doing to the soil, to our own bodies, to the divine feminine, and to women and girls. Drop all the way into your heart and perhaps become still enough to hear the voice of nature. Within each of us is something long forgotten. Welcome to the voyage of remembering who we are.

SOUL SOIL EXERCISES

Find a quiet place in nature to place your feet on the earth. This can be right outside your door, or, if you are in a city, perhaps find a nearby park. If this is impossible, place your feet anywhere and simply imagine dark, rich soil beneath them.

▶ Spend at least five minutes meditating on the interconnectedness of all things. What visuals and sensations come to mind? When you are done, freewrite for five to ten minutes. What wants to come through?

▶ Does anything come up in the form of resistance to the idea of being an interconnected part of nature? Are there any specific feelings in your body or thoughts in your mind related to this? Journal for at least five minutes about this.

▶ Looking around at your life, name at least three examples of the interconnectedness of all things. Where does interconnectedness show up in your day to day—for example, in the food you purchase and the water you drink? Where does it come from? What is the source?

PART TWO

THE CRY OF ALL WOMEN

Whatever that thing is where birth comes screaming into life and death exhales into eternity, we draw from that knowing and that power. We will not let our home burn. Not on our watch.

Now is the time to unite the soul and the world.[1]

RUMI

4

HOW DID
WE GET HERE?

I originally thought I was writing a book about soil health and climate change, but the journey brought me to the feet of the divine metaphor: the fertile soil is feminine. Destruction of the soil and destruction of the feminine go hand in hand. Addressing (and redressing) that violence means channeling the rage we feel around these longstanding injustices and transmuting that into peace.

In early 2017, long after I had completed the original manuscript of what you're reading now, I was talking to my dear friend and book doula, Monica, about where exactly the system got broken. How the hell did we get here? How could there possibly be such a huge blind spot with this many humans trying to figure out solutions to the climate crisis? How could the most obvious thing—the role of soil in the carbon cycle—be continuously overlooked by the experts? To be careening over the edge of existence and be this lost about the solution, humanity must have taken a wrong turn at some juncture.

I pulled my car over to the side of the road outside of Groundworks Coffee in Venice, CA, as Monica spoke about the roles of goddess history and private property. I knew nothing about goddess history, but something in my visceral memory leapt forward around private property. Having worked in the field of homelessness before graduate school, and having studied the human right to housing, I continued to run into the philosophical dead-end regarding private property, and without better resources to work through the intellectual morass, I eventually set the issue down. But when Monica mentioned it, something came roaring back. The concept of owning land was somehow tied to the concept of owning women, and, as an extension, owning people in general. As obvious as the connection between the Great Mother and climate catastrophe seems to me now, at the time the linkage between the goddess archetype and soil was just forming in my mind.

From that moment, I started to dig into the history of patriarchy. At first, I ran into all kinds of internet-troll-style slander around goddess history, as it seems the topic brings up all manner of suppressed rage in all sorts of people. When we consider our broken connection to the earth, the infinite, and ourselves, this actually isn't terribly surprising. And when we start to think about private property, we inevitably and appropriately run into the relationships of indigenous peoples with land, as well as the genocide, theft, oppression, and slavery occurring worldwide for thousands of years. It's not pretty, to say the least.

When the #metoo movement entered the picture and fundamentally shifted the prevailing conversation around sexual violence (primarily to non-male bodies), the tables began to turn and the arc of history was forever changed. People, particularly women, started to say *No. Time's up. This is unacceptable, and we won't tolerate it any longer.* The Harvey Weinstein moment was a year before the 2018 midterm elections, and the subsequent entrance of Alexandria Ocasio-Cortez, Greta Thunberg, and the youth climate movement (led primarily by teenage girls) to the international stage has been profound. This new class of young women has a message to deliver: the truth is unfuckwithable.

In early 2018, I gave a talk about soil and the interconnect-edness of all things, and I realized that there was no way to get around addressing patriarchy while doing so. But the moment that I prepared to talk about patriarchy, calling it by its name, I felt a sensation like an invisible hand grasping my throat. The more I leaned into it, the harder the hand would grasp. Rather than back down, I started speaking directly into it whenever I addressed any group, and, overwhelmingly, women began shar-ing a similar experience. We were all shocked at the bizarre and unmistakable sensation in our throats, a sensation I can now identify as embodied intergenerational trauma—a somatic col-lective memory of violence and silencing. Somehow my journey into soil health and climate change had taken me directly to the heart—and the voice—of the matter.

PATRIARCHY, EGO, SPIRIT

Writing about patriarchy while living in a patriarchical society is quite the paradox. It permeates every aspect of society, including the language we use to address it, as well as our intergenerational wounds and conditioning. It's fully alive in all of our most well-intentioned institutions, because it's fully alive in us. Writing this book required absolutely every ounce of courage I've been able to muster since its inception, because it requires me to let go of the armor that my PhD affords and strip off the muzzle of shame that silences women from discussing our embodied spiritual truths.

When this journey began, the story of soil was fairly obscure and has required a significant movement to bring it to the fore in the climate conversation. That was terrifying enough. My walk with Spirit and the divine feminine unfolding has been one of the most humbling and ego-defying processes I can imagine. At every turn, I've heard a toxic inner voice whispering "You can't do that," "You can't *say* that," "What will they think," "Get back in your box," "If you want to be accepted and respected, this is how it's done." It's the same voice that says "You'll go broke,"

"You'll be shunned," "You'll never find a partner (and having a partner defines you)," and even, "You'll die."

Sharing the truth is actually about power. True power. And we all have an inner critic that gets particularly loud when we decide to do something creative, daring, and true. I call mine the *curmudgeon*. I have found from personal experience (supported by the brilliant research of Brené Brown and others) that the light of vulnerability and authenticity are the best antidotes to shame. Shame has to live where it's dark, in the silence. Shame is about ego; creativity is about the soul. This journey—my story, this message—is about connection, love, vulnerability, and kindness. These are the medicines, the remedies for the stranglehold of patriarchy. Love always wins. In fact, it has already won.

I'm not going to dive into a mini-dissertation about patriarchy here. Nor will I say nearly enough about Spirit, witches, shamanism, plant medicine, or any of the like. Instead, I'm going to guide you through the basics, the simplest 101, solely for the purpose of connecting the dots. Instead of another lecture, what the world truly needs is gentle, loving guidance back to the truth, to ourselves, to one other, and to the earth. And who needs another argument about patriarchy anyway? In my experience, most of the time that just leads to more fighting, and the whole point here is that we need to stop fighting—ourselves and each other.

Stop and breathe. Imagine dropping roots into the ground and being held by the great biome of all of life in her diversity, including the insects, the plants, the fungi, the soils, and the trees. Feel how held you are by the Mother. Imagine dropping any thoughts that do not serve, including judgment and criticism, into the earth to be composted. Stay connected with your breath and feel into your body. Drop in to your heart. Breathe deeply.

While the story of patriarchy has always been played out most obviously by individuals and groups who have chosen to use force to gain and maintain control over others and over resources, the truth is that patriarchy lives in all of us. Patriarchy is the prison inside our own minds. It's the inner conditioning we express outwardly in relationships and societal institutions, and then re-internalize it once more, continuing the cycle. It's the voice of our ego's fear, rather than our soul's infinite being (Stephen Levine calls these "small mind" and "big mind," rather than ego and soul). Shame is its primary tool.

It's what keeps us small, scared, trapped, suppressed, unexpressed, exhausted, sick, mean, angry, bored, hiding, and depressed. It's the voice that tells us we're not good enough, we're not enough, there's never enough, and keeps us filling the void with external bullshit that only exacerbates our problems. It's what stops us from writing our book, singing our song, stepping into the spotlight. It's what gets us to compare ourselves to others and judge, hide, become jealous, procrastinate, sabotage ourselves and others, eat poorly, suppress our sacred sexuality, give away our power, hold shitty boundaries, communicate in unhealthy ways, be codependent, believe that play and creativity are frivolous, disrespect and misunderstand our bodies, and denigrate both the sacred masculine and the sacred feminine energies within ourselves. It tells us we need to earn our worth and drives us to achieve, prove, show off, control, exclude, and criticize in an attempt to gain worthiness. It's the resistance that Steven Pressfield names in *The War of Art: Break Through the Blocks and Win Your Inner Creative Battles* that kills creative work and inspires all manner of addictive behavior. It results in shallow breathing, poor sleep, stress, TMJ, IBS, inflammation, unhealthy bodies, excessive plastic surgery, addiction, over-medication, accidents, insecurity, and overall societal malaise.

That, my friends, is what's actually killing us. That's how we've been killing ourselves.

In simple terms, patriarchy is just the ego (the mind, the brain, etc.) trying to do its job. Its only job is to keep us alive, and to do so it does everything in its power to keep us safe. It means us no harm, but if we abide by it, we end up going through the motions of life, too afraid to step into anything we truly desire. Because this inner conditioning keeps us denying our highest, truest selves, it also drives us to turn on each other.

It's our soul—our highest self—that knows our infinite nature, transcends space and time, and wants us to expand, create, connect, and be love. Our soul is the part of us that innately knows and has always understood how nature (which is us) and the universe (also us) actually work, and what is needed to keep the entire system and ourselves in balance. Our soul is a piece of the benevolent, alive, co-creative universe expressed. Because the universe is made of love, so are we. This is why true self-love is the key to being grounded, integrated, and fully alive in our bodies.

All ancient systems of knowledge and wisdom passed down to us over thousands of years in some way offer these insights, but this understanding has always been within us. The wisdom of our bodies and our souls is infinite, and it's always readily available. We need only to tune in, listen, and drop in to our bodily sensations and inner knowing. Learning to do that and to trust in our personal knowing is the art of inner work and healing work.

Our own heartbeat is the drumbeat.

Revolutionizing our relationship to the soil and healing from the ground up requires that we turn to the tools of transformative healing (which can include Western psychology, depth psychology, Eastern medicine and modalities, indigenous practices, self-study, ceremony, etc.). The only way to unravel patriarchy and untangle ourselves from its mess is to look into ourselves, because the truth lives within each of us. Rather than battle with the ego, our work is to integrate, become aware of ego, love it for what it is, thank it, and remember who we truly are. The truth is infinite, universal love, and that includes self-love. The only way through is to find self-love and forgive each other and ourselves.

THE GREAT MOTHER AND THE INVITATION OF OUR TIME

According to some, our connection to the land, Spirit, each other, and our bodies, as well as to the subconscious and dream states, began to break down around five thousand years ago. Some place it about two to three thousand years ago, closer to the advent of Christianity, but the beginning of the dismantling, deconstruction, and co-optation of the goddess archetypes happened quite some time before then. Co-optation is the act of taking over something original, distorting it, and passing it off as your own—a favorite pastime of institutional patriarchy.

As it turns out, the first creation stories around the world started with the Great Mother—Shakti (India, 9000 BCE), Kokyangwuti (the spider grandmother of the Hopi, time unknown), Ataensic (Huron, time unknown), Houtu (China, time unknown), Inanna (Sumer, 4000 BCE), Ishtar (Babylon, 4000 BCE), Hathor (Egypt, 2400 BCE), Isis (Egypt, 2400 BCE), Aditi (India, 1700 BCE), Papatuanuku (Maori, 1500 BCE), Asherah (Canaan, 1200 BCE), Astarte (Syria, 1200 BCE), Gaia (Greece, 1400 BCE), Demeter (Greece, 1400 BCE), Aphrodite (Cyprus, 1000 BCE), and Pachamama (Andes, 1000 BCE) to name a few. The Great Mother in all of her forms oversees and embodies life, magic, fertility, agriculture, birth, death, love, beauty, sexuality, war, women, pleasure, desire, passion, nature, and the earth.

Goddess archetypes are nonlinear, some springing from older versions, some holding space for new ones. The Great Mother (including the dark goddess archetype) was worshipped worldwide as the primordial cosmic universal energy, the creator and destroyer of life, goddess of birth and death, overseer of fertility of the soil. Life and death came from and returned to the soil through food and our bodies. We see the life-death-rebirth cycle also reflected in the seed metaphor: life gestates in the darkness, springs forth in birth, grows, blossoms, and eventually returns to the earth in death to nourish new life (as compost, ahem).

Conversely, most of us have been taught that the earth is just dirt, that it's base, filthy, a low form of matter, and that the material it's made of is the root of all evil. Hell is typically placed under the earth, after all. And as it happens, the Latin root word for *matter* means "mother."

Welcome to the underworld journey. Back to our collective blind spot. Climate change is directly connected to the suppression of feminine sexuality, which is part of all of us, as every human embodies the dance of feminine and masculine energies. The fertile soil is the key to the great mysteries of the divine and our path toward healing. And our fearful, controlling, codependent relationship with the earth and each other (rather than a healthy interdependency) fuels capitalism, patriarchy, and the climate emergency. Everything is connected.

Each of us carries this ancient wound. And at the same time, we are all inherently whole. We have access to everything we need to heal, we just need the courage to fully face it head on and to feel, forgive, and integrate it. We can and must help each other through this spiritual journey of a lifetime, remembering and returning to the void from which we come. The pain of patriarchy has been fed and passed through our subconscious programming for generations—all the mother and father wounds we carry are intergenerational. Healing the Great Mother requires intergenerational healing, individually and collectively. When we heal something within ourselves, we heal the lines for eternity from the past, in the present, and into the future. When we choose to stop the line of trauma within ourselves, we transmute the pain that has been passed down unconsciously from parents and society to children into love. And when we share this loving work with our children and others, it ripples into the future. This is the invitation of our time.

5

THE CRY OF
ALL WOMEN

I n early 2015, I was talking to a
friend about an ayahuasca ceremony I had recently attended,
and she asked if I had heard any screaming. I didn't think I had,
but she said, "Oh, in my ceremony, I heard this one woman
scream. It was the cry of all women." I shuddered. I've never
given birth, but I have some innate sense of what she meant.
In fact, those words have been burned into my psyche and my
body ever since, and some echo of the cry of all women continues to reverberate through my spirit.

There is an aching scream from the center of the universe.
Against all that stands. Against my own resistance. Against
everything that does not serve. The scream from within me
says this will not stand. This will not stand. Not on my fucking watch.

For all the newborns who arrived in 2020. For all who came
before and who will follow after. For those who will become
the mothers and fathers of the future. For anyone who has ever
been, the cry pours out of me from some unknown depth: I will
not stand here and let our home burn before my eyes. Humanity
is not going down on our watch.

Not. On. My. Watch.

We have had enough. As the mothers and fathers of this planet, our duty is to protect the sacred and say no to those seeking to destroy it, and say yes to all the things we are growing from, learning, and creating through transmuting and alchemizing the pain. To protect the sick, elderly, young, disabled, poor, and disadvantaged. To care for the animal, plant, and fungi kingdoms, and all of the earth's interrelated systems. To end sexual assault, harassment, and trafficking. To stand for future generations. To heal the lasting wounds of indigenous cultures and lands with each other. To stand, for now and eternity, for the highest good of all. With kindness, humility, grace, and love.

Allow me to guide you through the terrain of the dark goddess—the exiled, forgotten, banished, suppressed, and oppressed part of the collective psyche that holds the keys to our greatest collective challenges and opportunities. She is Cybele (Phrygia, time unknown), Lilith (Mesopotamia, time unknown), Mór-Ríoghain (Ireland, time unknown), Coatlicue (Mesoamerica, 1300 BCE), Hecate (Greece, 1400 BCE), Nyx (Greece, 1400 BCE), Persephone (Greece, 1400 BCE), Durga (India, time unknown), Kali (India, time unknown), and Sekhmet (Egypt, 2400 BCE), as well as Hera (Greece, 1400 BCE), Hestia (Greece, 1400 BCE), and Demeter (Greece, 1400 BCE) in their original forms. She is the primal void that gives life to all things, the original mother, the crone, the moon, the night sky, priestess of the sacred fires of sexual healing, desire, connection to feminine independence, and the earth herself. She is the drumbeat of the goddess, the primordial sound, the blood of each mother's heartbeat, the source, the origin. In her banishment, we have banished ourselves. In her suppression, we have suppressed the only thing that allows us to truly understand ourselves as part of the cycles of nature. And by forgetting her, we have forgotten who we truly are, along with our worthiness and our power to heal ourselves.

The answer to the most dreadful challenge humankind has ever faced does not live in the rational mind. She lives in the shadows. In the dark recesses of our own psyches, in long lost archetypes, in the collective unseen underground. In the mud, in the soil. In the fertile darkness where life thrives and forms and dies and reorganizes and rebirths to live again. She is the forest floor. The mushrooms. The dank, sweet smell of life and death. She lives in the space between, the space unseen. She is pussy, she is placenta, she is menstrual blood, she is muse, she is mother, grandmother, and goddess.

She has been pushed, prodded, criminalized, cursed, denied, sold, held captive, defiled, mutilated, tortured, oppressed, burned, and killed en masse. She has been rewritten, co-opted, erased, ridiculed, cast aside, gaslighted, belittled, desacralized, and bullied. She has been turned into temptress, seductress, evil witch, devil worshipper, freak, demoness, dark poison, drug, siren, hag, property, vengeful jealous wife, and threat to all that is holy and good.

She is the fertile soil. She welcomes the seed, envelops its gestation, and holds holy space for birth. Life springs forth from her and she nourishes its roots. She lives in constant exchange with all that is. And when we sleep, when we pass, when we cross over, she welcomes us back. She oversees the transition. She is the great inhale. She is the garden. She is the Great Mother. The yin. And she is holding us gently in facing our shame, grief, disconnection, and rage, welcoming us back in our darkest hour.

To face her is to face ourselves. To humbly face our own darkness, our own suppression, our own shadow and confusion. Our own fragmentation and denial. Our own sacred sexuality, our own death, our own voice, our own freedom, our own power. She is our pleasure, ecstasy, grief, and rage all at once. She invites us to remember our inherent value and our power as embodied parts of the living, ever-unfolding universe. Sacred geometry spills from her skirt folds. She is nature herself, and she whispers to us that we are part of her. That we have always known. That we have everything we could possibly need. That she is infinitely abundant and we are forever safe when we walk with her. Patriarchy cannot, and will not, stand in her integrated presence.

Women—the cycles of our bodies, of menstruation and childbirth and life and death (for all of us who do and do not bleed)—are intimately tied to the cycles of nature, of the seasons, the moon, and harvest. So many of us feel thoroughly connected to the great unknown, and yet we also know that we can't run around saying these things to just anybody. In our disconnection, our deepest worthiness wound, which has been passed down through generations from the time we lost our connection with the Great Mother, leads to our unsustainable relationship with the earth. So much of what we are looking for externally in our capitalistic world actually lies within this original mother wound. When we forget that we are inherently worthy, the whole system thrives on our feeling incomplete, seeking approval and love from elsewhere. But what if the devil and the underworld are in fact simply the realm of the human unconscious, neither good nor bad? And what if inherent worthiness is the opposite of original sin? What if we are, in fact, the fruits and blossoms of the tree of life?

When we love our bodies, we connect to food and love the earth. When we spend time meditating on the 100 trillion cells that make up each of our bodies, the trillions of atoms that make up those cells, and all the spaces between, we can perhaps let go of some of our attachments and stop for a moment to simply be in awe of what we are made of. When we connect and turn inward, we can unpack the mysteries of being and living.

Conversely, as we struggle against ourselves and each other, the illusion of separateness drives us into a maddening amnesia about how things actually work and what is really going on here. This is not woo. It's a perspective based on empirical evidence. Here's simple truth: all life is one. Here's another simple truth: we take ourselves way too fucking seriously. If we could just stand down for a moment and breathe it in, we could see what's right in front of our faces. We are soil. Soil is life.

We can't see the forest for the trees. As we are unconsciously thrashing about our lives, many of us are starting to get the sense that there may be a greater truth out there. Reaching this truth has required us to slow down, get quiet, and take a giant step back. Perhaps we have been standing *on* the truth all along. What if the simplest solution on the planet is beneath our feet? Wouldn't that be a trip? Some part of us resists the idea that it could be that simple, but what if it were? Perhaps we can open ourselves to the possibility that this world is not always what it seems, and that our illusions are—literally and figuratively—the root of our problems.

> Wherever you go in the world, whatever
> animal, plant, blob you look at, if it is
> alive, it will use the same dictionary and
> know the same code. All life is one.[1]
>
> MATT RIDLEY

Welcome to the "persistent flawed thought that we are separate from the world," as MIT-trained artist and scientist Jeff Lieberman puts it.[2] The separation we perceive is utter nonsense. Just nonsense. Lieberman recommends that we see the entire world as our own body. If we could see this truth more clearly, how would we behave differently? To be fair, as lovely as that notion is, most of us have been trained to trash our bodies in the same manner we treat the earth, so maybe it's a matter of compassion: if we were more compassionate with our bodies, would we be more compassionate with the earth? The revolution will not be patriarchal. It will be (and already is) fiercely feminine.

WHAT HAPPENED TO THE GODDESS?

Humans lived and loved long before the invention of the written word, and history before the written word is subject to debate and interpretation. Proving an exact history of what happened to the goddess with a bunch of citations is not the point here, and the goddess herself has nothing to prove. She speaks through dreams, intergenerational memory, visions, mythology, movement, oral tradition, ceremony, whispers of nature, poetry, and vibration, and she simply does not play by patriarchy's rules.

It's worth noting that academia has been patriarchal from its onset, and its manner of controlling the conversation about research (as well as who gains access to participate) has particular consequences for all of us. Fear of feminine intuition, nonlinear thought, and embodied knowing has been alive and well in most rooms I've ever entered (although thankfully I had wonderfully supportive mentors and committee members), and our job is to face this resistance and mend it with love. We all know that history is written by the dominant party, and culture is ultimately shaped by its conquerors. Reclaiming our stories and unearthing suppressed histories is an essential aspect of our healing.

Here's the thing: the ubiquitous existence of the Great Mother in all her forms around the world, thousands and thousands of years before Christianity, is not something anyone debates. At the same time, we stand at the edge of extinction because our relationship to ourselves, the earth, and the goddess has gone missing in our collective consciousness. The soil itself—as a critical part of the climate conversation—is also glaringly absent in mainstream thought. Something is clearly going on here.

THE GRANDMOTHERS SPEAK

I started opening my throat chakra in a guided ceremony in May 2018. In that moment, I realized that I couldn't sing a peep of anything, even in a completely safe space, without bawling my eyes out. My voice—my song—was completely repressed.

Not long ago, one of my teachers introduced me to *A Call to Power: The Grandmothers Speak, Book 1* by Sharon McErlane.[3] Here, the grandmothers—elders from all traditions—guide us all back to balancing the yin on this earth. They remind us of the feminine principle, the fertile soil—how to root and how to release. The grandmothers also guide us to trust ourselves and never force ourselves (or any plant or animal) to grow too fast. To each its own pace. They return us to ceremony, play, joy, beauty, and the sacredness of all life. With kindness, patience, and humor, they remind us of our place in the fabric of being, and encourage us to let go of judgment and attachment and to pray together. They utilize the tree of life to remind us of the balance between in-breath and out-breath, receiving and giving, rooting and rising, mother and father, yin and yang. They help us feel the connection through our underground root network to all places and peoples of the earth, to each other and all life in a web of interconnectedness. We open the net of light by breathing into this web with peaceful, loving intention.

So we breathe deeply. Drop in. Imagine the root systems beneath our feet and the connections between us all. Feel our hearts beating and the love that runs through everything. *Remember*, the grandmothers whisper.

JUNO, VESTA, AND LILITH

Older versions of goddess archetypes are found in odd places, and only then with some digging. In the last couple of years, a few have called out to me, namely Juno and Vesta, whom I learned about through Chani Nicholas's goddess astrology course.

I was shocked to find that the Roman Juno (Greek Hera) was originally an independent triple-moon goddess representing the merging of spirit with matter, with no partner before the patriarchy introduced Jupiter (Greek Zeus) into her story. In indigenous pre-Hellenic Greece, Hera was an original Mother Goddess and her marriage to Zeus was forced during the patriarchal takeover.[4] Their unhappy marriage is famously known for Zeus's raping, shape-shifting, and philandering, and Hera's jealousy and acting out without leaving the marriage. This rewrite of the story represents the suppression of women, the matriarchy, and goddess religions, as well as the colonization of an indigenous population and takeover of their spiritual landscape. The marriage itself represents a forced transition from nonmonogamous rites and rituals to monogamous marriage as a means to secure patrilineal control of land and resources. Gender norms in this region were also forced from a state of fluidity into patriarchy's binary shape during these times. Perhaps it's no accident that roofies, hazing, gaslighting, and rape culture play the roles they do in "Greek" fraternities today.

It had never occurred to me before to question that narrative and look into the pre-Hellenic history of these archetypes and stories. I hadn't the slightest idea how powerful and important archetypes are in the collective and individual psyche, and, like most of us, I merely accepted what I was taught by mainstream Western culture. Archetypes are behind how we view and understand ourselves in the world, which explains why marketers and advertisers use them so expertly to sell us products and inform us how to view our bodies and relationships. In *Not All Dead White Men: Classics and Misogyny in the Digital Age*, Donna Zuckerberg unpacks this relationship with the ancient world and how it affects racism and institutionalized rape culture today. The co-optation of the goddess was an ancient power grab, with an immeasurable legacy to this day. Our stories define our reality.

I also came to learn that the Roman Vesta (Greek Hestia), goddess of hearth and home, keeper of the sacred flame of the community, overseer of the Vestal Virgins, was forcibly removed from her priestesses. The word *virgin* once meant "woman unto herself," and it referred to priestesses of sacred sexual healing. The distance we now feel between sexuality and spirituality is a testament to this disjuncture. The Virgins were separated from their sexual healing role and given political and financial power if they vowed to abstain from sex, essentially becoming what we now understand as nuns. Vesta's name was eventually incorporated into the word *investment*.[5] Here, the splitting of an archetype translates into real-world changes that have everything to do with control of resources, land, people, sexuality, and spirituality. It's no coincidence that the suppression of reproductive rights and education in women and girls around the world has a direct link to the climate emergency. When women and girls have access to education and sexual and reproductive rights, their lives can thrive along with their communities. With so many women and girls currently trapped in poverty with more children than they desire and without access to education, we can see how this sexual autonomy wound lies at the heart of the climate crisis, along with the soil.

Through the examples of Juno and Vesta, we can see how the goddess is replaced by a paradigm that does not honor the sacred sexual, the independent woman, indigenous spirituality, or the land. The ties among fertility, sexuality, the feminine, the moon, the earth, and their related cycles became fragmented and lost. And sexuality, women, and the earth began to be connected with sin, guilt, and shame instead. This brings me to Lilith.

Perhaps one of the most defiled characters in goddess archetypal history, Lilith was Adam's first wife, an equal partner, and *made of the same earth*. In the Christian takeover of the story, Lilith was expelled from the garden for not being sexually subservient to Adam, and then Eve was created from Adam's rib.

Lilith was threatened with a curse: if she didn't submit to Adam, she would have a thousand babies a day and watch them all die. Instead of choosing to live as a subservient partner, Lilith made the terribly difficult choice to preserve feminine autonomy and suffer the consequences, thus rejecting patriarchal control. To this day, Christianity views Lilith as a threat, presenting her as a demon goddess who eats unborn children (the imagery depicts her as a gruesome demon or witch). In her example, we see yet again how the dark goddess was destroyed, vilified, exiled, co-opted, and punished to upend her natural universal power, her story rewritten to keep patriarchy's rules in place. Lilith, in fact, stands for feminine strength and actually oversees the care of unborn babies. She's a fierce energy—a protector and a reminder of choice, power, and truth.

THE VAGINA-VOICE CONNECTION

Lilith also holds space for women to heal the *other woman wound* in Western culture. She invites us to step all the way into our power, our choice, our voice, rather than buy into the belief that our power can be stripped from us if we lose a man's approval. Lilith is not enraged, bitter, or jealous, as the patriarchal rewrite would have us believe. She also takes no shit. Her *no* is sacred, as is her *fuck yes* (I'll return to these boundaries in part five). This scares the crap out of the patriarchal egoic mind and lies at the base of our most intensely buried fears and wounds. Lilith does not get bullied or manipulated. In other words, Lilith is a fucking badass. She *is* the garden.

My own journey brought me directly into this wound and the healing light beyond it. After the throat chakra ceremony rocked me to my core, I entered a process of opening my sacral chakra, particularly with regard to my sexuality. Once again, I found myself in a puddle of tears when faced with my own repression when invited to expand here. I first resisted working with a guide at all, because some part of me knew what I was up against: a lifetime (perhaps multiple lifetimes) of conditioning around monogamy, relationships, love, desire, exploration, pleasure, and my body. I also knew my body and my higher self were calling for something greater.

The Sanskrit word for the sacral chakra, *Svadhisthana*, means "in her own abode," referring to the sacral or "holy" bone as the home of Kundalini, the divine mother. Remember that the fertile soil requires moisture—who knew the soil book would lead me here? The soil is, in fact, sexy. I write this from a place of delicious opening, and I have walked through firewalls of fear to find my way in this part of my healing journey.

It started with the clear intuitive guidance to work with an individual that I knew would invite me *way* out of my comfort zone. I squeamishly resisted that inner nudge for as long as I could, but ultimately I knew I had a doorway and a choice. With some deep breaths and ego deaths, I reached out to my guide. In a moment that I now view as truly comical, he introduced a choice (as an exercise to get out of my comfort zone) between participating in a threesome, orgy, or dominatrix encounter. I had twenty-four hours to decide.

For someone who thought of herself as fairly sexually open and adventurous, I was shocked at the complete brick wall I hit within myself. I wept, agonized, and tried to bargain with myself, and my ego invented every scenario imaginable about how I would be harmed, hurt, rejected, and experience more trauma. Thankfully, I was working with someone who both ensured my safety and invited me to push way, way beyond what I imagined I was capable of. At the absolute last moment, I picked the orgy option. Hilariously, one of my friends started introducing me as "Erin, who is organizing an orgy." Immediately, people wanted to be invited to the orgy I was somehow now responsible for (the one I thought I was just "attending").

Once I'd said yes, it was like unlocking some kind of super-power. I was amused and bewildered, and still a little terrified.

As the whole adventure unfolded, it became clear that there were aspects in each of the three proposed choices inviting me to look into unclaimed parts of myself—my initiatory masculinity, my suppressed desire to explore with women, and the other woman wound mentioned above. As I leaned into my yes about this orgy decision, I began to have Kundalini openings, which felt like rainbow disco ice cream running through my body. I found that when I was in this embodied, contained energy, I could somehow meet and dissolve patriarchal creepiness just by being. A guy who whistled at me from his bike nearly crashed it when I alchemized and owned the energy as I kept walking, and a sketchy guy I met at a bar somehow morphed into a gentleman.

The orgy took a few months to materialize. It turned out to be an exquisitely held and curated event of group exploration, and it was one of the most mind-blowingly wonderful experiences of my life. I felt beautiful, held, whole, alive, safe, and fully embodied in the feminine essence. Perhaps the most unexpected gift of it all was the sound of multiple women enjoying themselves sexually. I had no idea what I had been missing out on for most of my adult life, because I'd been living behind a wall of fear and shame and guilt I didn't even know was there. Happy pussy, like the fertile soil, requires ample moisture and attention.

I realized, even in my late thirties, that every time I felt desire rise up in me, I subconsciously responded with an internal *no* that I had learned some time in adolescence. Having internalized society's fears, rules, and shame (as well as the shame of so many others around me), I hardly knew my true *fuck yes*. Before this time in my life, I'd actually felt pretty good in my own sexuality, but I had no idea what possibilities were beyond the next door. I started to combine my sexual exploration with sensuality practices, as well as working with the magic of the menstrual cycle. I reread *Pussy: A Reclamation* by luminary Mama Gena (Regena Thomashauer), a powerfully activating classic in the field of women's empowerment, and at every juncture where I felt like I just could not take another step, I took another step.

I've now explored nonmonogamous relationships, I've profoundly healed friendships with exes through newfound openness and compassion, and I've arrived at a new place where I encourage and celebrate the unlocking of everyone's sacred sexuality. In love, relationships, and pure enjoyment, I've walked through invisible walls of my own past creation to find the joy, gentleness, and an unbridled release I'd never experienced before. My greatest fears—rejection, separation, and not being good enough—became glittering doorways to my deepest relationships, joy, sex, and love. In spiritual growth, this is the way.

In this journey, I came across another blind spot: the *vagina-voice connection*. My discovery was facilitated by a dear friend whose work focuses on feminine sexuality and the voice, as well as my own explorations with my throat chakra and its connective paths in my own body. The Latin root word *cervix* means "neck." Our breath is connected to our pelvic floor, and our entire nervous system is connected through the vagus nerve. A calming vibration in our throat can calm our whole body. More research is unfolding around the vagina-brain connection.[5] For example, we now know that whole body orgasms (rather than genital-focused) are not only possible, but that we can access them in an ecstatic way to heal our whole system. Similar to the profound effect of gut health on our moods, immune systems, and overall well-being, our sacral center is connected to female hormones, moods, and intuition.[6]

I've learned from my own experience that simple humming can calm my entire system—our pleasure, our sense of well-being, and our voices are all connected—and I have also come to learn that pleasure is my birthright, that I have everything I need within myself. When we live in a stiff, controlling, hyper-intellectualized, fear-driven world, we tend to disconnect from our bodies and true voices. In a world run by fear, our cries are muzzled and silenced. It's no wonder that we find ourselves so lost as a collective and so divorced from the simplest truths about our bodies and well-being.

Again, the more I share these experiences, the more women related their own pain (emotional, physical, and psychic). Women are circling up to open the honest conversation with each other. Our unconscious disconnection from our voices and our sexuality is part of the legacy of our disconnection from the Great Goddess. The cry of all women, the terrible pain from these unknown depths, is arising from the depths of this injustice. Our voice is our birthright. Our sexuality is our birthright. Both are our connection to Spirit, ourselves, each other, and the earth. Intergenerational suppression has us denying our truths and passing the wound of silence on to each other, until we decide to break the chain. My relationship to jealousy, competition, using my voice in sex, and exploration have all been completely transformed, and I'm still learning all the time. With great courage comes great reward, and the goddess is always here, inviting us along.

The truth can be painful at first, but also liberating once we begin to integrate it. Let us be gentle with ourselves and each other as the truth arises. We have all played a part in creating the situation we find ourselves in as humans. As we begin to see and remember, we can breathe life into the new world that is possible. To integrate these truths, we can rely on our own gentle inner work, journaling, sharing, laughing, and crying.

SOUL SOIL EXERCISES

▶ Take at least ten minutes in a private, comfortable space and drop in to your body and feel what's there. Feel into all sensations (pain, itching, tension, etc.) and notice any thoughts that come up. How does your nervous system feel (wired, frayed, calm)? How does your stress level feel (high, medium)? What does your inner monologue say? Feel into any pain you might be feeling. Without judging or attaching, breathe into these spaces and journal for at least five minutes about what comes up. When you're done, hum for at least another five minutes to release your energy further. Practice this exercise once a day for a week and see what changes. Begin to replace every *no* that comes up with a *yes* and every negative thought with an *I love you*.

▶ Reflect on your relationship with the Great Goddess and goddess archetypes. Begin to reflect on how these themes and archetypes show up in your life.

UNTANGLING THE PATRIARCHY IN OURSELVES: GRIEF AND RAGE

Recognizing that the patriarchy exists within us is the first step to healing, and healing ourselves is the essential ingredient to healing the planet. Light work; shadow work; healing the sister wound; reconnecting to plants and the earth; reconnecting to ceremony, ritual, and sound; healing our relationship with money; and reconnecting to our bodies, sacred sexuality, and the creative life force of the universe are all necessary to create the world we want. From the inside out, we can rethink, reorganize, and re-imagine a healthy world and regenerative society into being. Our organizations and institutions—built on the strong foundation of a regenerative food system and a zero waste (circular) economy—must reflect the inner balance and harmony that we can find only from going within. We must inquire into the thoughts on repeat in our heads, the same force-fed thoughts that shape our perceptions and create our reality. To do this, we get to rely on the nourishing and anti-patriarchal practices of movement, meditation, self-love, and self-care.

The most formidable challenge I've found in the ongoing journey of unraveling the patriarchy within myself lies in healing my reactionary reflex and pointing the finger at others. Blame itself is a patriarchal act. The truth is that those of us expressing the fear-based ego the most aggressively are in tremendous suffering —expressing hatred, perpetuating fear, and enacting more violence, greed, and control simply means that we are far, far away from our highest soul selves. We are all together in this grand process, in the oneness of all things, no matter how dark and separate we may seem in a given moment and experience. And this has been the case throughout the history of humanity.

In the face of abject violence, harm, destruction, hatred, and even low-level pettiness, judgment, cynicism, competition, and unhealthy attachment in the world, it's hard not to point fingers. Even when we know that peace and love are the answer, we can still feel an overwhelming urge to set fire to the unjust world and destroy it. It feels good to be right, to yell about what and who is wrong. Tear shit down! Burn it! Destroy them! I know. I feel it, too.

The only way forward is to face the ego within ourselves. Diving into the inner work to face ourselves can bring a lot up—old wounds that need us to witness and integrate them. At first it can be disorienting and uncomfortable. Up until now, many of us have been stopping short of self-work because we are avoiding all the pain sitting just below the surface. But the pain is there to educate us, to direct us toward what we can heal within. In fact, at every turn, the pain is an invitation and an opening into knowing ourselves more deeply, and possibly finding a new form of joy on the other side.

Our confusion about the cycles of life and nature (which, again, includes humans) can only happen if the patriarchy keeps its illusions and violence in place. Hence, all the rage that patriarchy inspires. We've all externalized and re-internalized many aspects of patriarchy and at best are actively at work deprogramming and decolonizing our own minds, work, and systems. It's maddening to understand how much we are fighting ourselves from within and then projecting our internal struggles onto others. Unfortunately, most of us still don't understand this and are walking around with all kinds of toxic programming that keep us continuing broken systems that are destroying the earth, ourselves, and each other. This is the juncture where self-care, inner work, and spiritual inquiry and practice come into play. The outer reflects the inner and vice versa. The health (or lack thereof) of the planet reflects our inner health: physical, psychological, emotional, and spiritual.

How do we fight for the good without blame, and how do we find peace without spiritual bypassing? I've found that radical responsibility is the only way, because the world is a reflection of what's happening inside of us. I stumble every day. The path is truly humbling. The ego is quick, sticky, and slippery, and it will do anything to keep us in fear, comparison, blame, and criticism to keep itself in control. Naming injustice, speaking the truth, holding ourselves and others accountable to the best of our ability, and working to change systems that uphold the egoic, fear-based patriarchy is the way. But the way is also facing ourselves with compassion day after day, deprogramming our own fear-based conditioning. As within, so without. One does not work or exist fully without the other.

Living a soul-filled, love-expanding, open, empowering life of personal freedom is an every day, every moment embodied practice. Leaning into an economic system that provides opportunity for all to choose a life that aligns with the earth is fundamentally critical. Our choices in terms of what we eat, our relationship with the earth, what we purchase, how we travel, and how we treat others are all reflections of our inner state. We can only truly transform the world for good by transforming ourselves. Along the way, we get to dismantle what no longer serves us (or never did to begin with), as well as create the new world systems in its place.

Truly living in a state of non-judgment, non-attachment, and inner peace is our path to the peaceful world that is possible. Showing up and observing and forgiving our toxic thought forms is the way to dismantle patriarchy from the inside out. Pull on this thread and the whole sweater unravels. Patriarchy and capitalism can only continue in a toxic soup of unkind thoughts, so remembering our inherent worthiness—our birthright as children of this planet—is essential.

Imagine for a moment a world society operating from a fully-expressed, soul-fulfilling, love-based place. Just imagine. Breathe. Feel the resistance. Breathe again. And imagine. It's so beautiful. Love first. Hearts open. Personal expression. Sexual healing. Balance with the earth. Abundant regeneration. Social equity. Dignity. Freedom. Music. Art. Play. Institutions that reflect our true desires. Imagine.

How did humans exist before the collective scales tipped in favor of patriarchy? Was life some giant blissfest? Who knows? The ego, of course, has always been around, and will continue to be here, so rather than destroy the ego, we dance with it. Love it. Thank it for working to protect us. And gently return to our soul's greatest expression—love. Collectively, the idea is not to idealize the past or attempt to create some sort of political global utopia; the idea is to tap into the actual bliss available to us at all times—found in connection with our soul, Spirit, source energy—and to create from there.

SOUL SOIL EXERCISES

Find a quiet place where you can set aside between five and ten minutes. Take five deep breaths. Let yourself sit with any grief and or rage that comes up when feeling into the presence of patriarchy. Allow anything that you might not initially want to look at or feel to come up. Journal for as long as feels good and free-write on the following questions:

▶ Where do you find patriarchy showing up in your life? What comes up when you start thinking about it?

▶ Find a way to physically express these feelings in private (my favorites include primal screaming into a pillow in a parked car, punching a pillow in a parked car, crying, running, and dancing).

▶ Identify ten places in your life where you can untangle yourself from patriarchal ways of being and replace fear with love. Keep your list in a journal or place where you can revisit it as a self-check-in.

To support this work, try some of the free heart-healing meditations on my website. Another wonderful way to start moving this energy is to find a community to share it with. Find your community by asking around or by searching online.

PART THREE

HEALING FROM THE GROUND UP

Finding our feet on the ground and finding our energetic roots is the first step to healing from the ground up.

6

INNER WORK AND
OUTER WORK ARE ONE

Find all four corners of each foot on the earth (outdoors if possible, but anywhere will do). Take three long, deep, cleansing breaths. Scan your body for anything that does not serve you and imagine releasing it into the earth, where Mother Nature can compost it and turn it into something more useful. No matter what is going on in the outside world, our inner state is up to us. With simple grounding, breath, and mindset techniques, we can meet anything going on inside of us with love and tranquility.

I started a light yoga practice as well as Western therapy in my late twenties while in graduate school. Yoga helped my body relax from long hours in front of a computer, and I treated it primarily as exercise and a mode of unwinding. My first therapist handed me a book called *Lovingkindness: The Revolutionary Art of Happiness* by Sharon Salzberg. I was immediately mesmerized—the book helped me disarm and untangle some heated social conflicts in my life right away just by managing my perspective and inner state. I employed Salzberg's mediations and mindfulness techniques to guide myself away from the world of intellectual control and to lessen my tendency to grip onto external experiences. At the same time in yoga, I remember feeling astonished at the sense of peace and calm I experienced during savasana each time. Competitive athletics in high school and college had always kept my body balanced with academic work; even so, I remember constantly feeling exhausted. Everything in my life (with the exception of the few years I spent solo traveling) had been about exceling, pushing, achieving, and winning at something. Like so many of us, I found myself on a trajectory of achievement and productivity that seemed to be a train with no brakes. Whatever this force was, it wanted me to be well-liked (but not intimidating), to look good (within certain parameters), to be sought after sexually (but not overtly so), to marry well and bear children (at which point I would hand over my autonomy and sexuality), to make as much money as humanly possible with a good and respectable job title, and no matter what to have a solid 401K and an excellent image.

Essentially, my entire task in life was to avoid rejection by anybody or anything, and thus to keep my egoic sense of safety intact by maintaining an unassailable image and never take any risks. I spent a good part of my life playing along, resisting, rebelling, running away, and otherwise reacting to this utterly unwinnable set of demands.

Just before I turned thirty, I left a six-year relationship and devoted myself to a process of finding my authentic self. Through this process of discovery, I've found layer after layer of conditioning, and I've spent years exploring what feels like every modality toward my own wellness through personal and spiritual growth. This has gone hand in hand with my unfolding relationship with nature, the food I eat, and nourishing modalities like yoga. Healing from the ground up takes a number of forms, and I realize now that every breath I took in every yoga class (leading up to teacher training in Bali) was gently guiding me back to Spirit, back to myself, and back to Mother Nature. I thought I was relaxing and doing something that felt good for my body, but it turns out that moving with attention to the breath is actually more profound. It's the same with gentle meditation, going to a farmer's market, or taking care of a plant indoors.

What we truly need in our personal lives is a mirror of what we need worldwide. As we create a regenerative world, we create regenerative lives for ourselves. Imagine what that might be like: taking the time and space to replenish our personal well without guilt, shame, or ridicule. The human spirit, body, and mind need constant nourishment in order for us to create outwardly.

Imagine a water well. If we take and take from that well, it will eventually dry up. We need to give it time to naturally replenish so that it can keep providing water for us. Now imagine the earth. The same concept holds true. The earth naturally replenishes and finds balance, and it's up to us to work with her and provide this space. It requires zero effort. The system naturally rights itself and finds alignment and balance when we only take what we need. It's the magic of Mother Nature.

I've found through my process of healing from the ground up that inner work and outer work are actually one and the same. I've found that working with plants and the soil, beginning to heal my relationship with indigenous peoples and lands, working with plant medicine, and working to create a more just and equitable society are integral to the healing of my soul. Yoga, meditation, breathwork, and mindset inquiry all aid in my healing of relationships and in infusing love into anything my hands touch. As gardening teaches me patience (as I mentioned before, the grandmothers make it clear that no plant or human should ever be rushed), I've learned that fighting and controlling in the name of creating a better world are not the way. Yes, the injustices are innumerable and nearly incomprehensible in their reach. Still, for me, the path requires co-creating lovingly with Mother Nature and trusting her guidance and the alignment of all things. While our minds feel certain that we must create, move, and break things with brute force, the Great Mother asks us to surrender and flow in a dance of inspired acting, releasing, and receiving.

The results of following this wisdom in my life have been nothing short of magical. What has become abundantly clear to me is that the way we're taught to treat ourselves is the way we as a species have been mining the earth. We are currently living in the last vestiges of an extractive system, both in our relationship with the earth and in our relationship to our personal well-being. What would it look like instead to be in balance instead of endlessly taking? What would it look like to give back?

Breathe. None of this is actually work. Not hard work the way we've been trained to believe the nature of work is. Facing our inner fears is real. And often uncomfortable. At the same time, the yin is about receiving. Yes, we face the brass tacks. Yes, we go back to the basics. And at the same time Mother Nature is imploring us to receive what is already here. What always has been with us. The abundance of the earth herself. Regeneration. What do we do in the world to create the vision we so desire? We roll up our sleeves and celebrate.

As embodied souls, we have things to do in the material world. Healing soil all over the world is no small task. At the same time, it can be joyous, especially when we have a larger perspective on what we are up to with regard to human consciousness. As we remember and integrate the Mother Goddess—as we remember and integrate rejected parts of ourselves—we can work with the earth herself to create positive feedback loops that will right the system. Virtuous circles.

The burning questions are: What do we do, specifically? And how do we do it? My answer is as follows: We must do both the inner work and the outer work to get to where we are going. The inner work requires going inward to search for the self and deprogram the misunderstandings we have of ourselves that keep us locked in these hopelessly failing systems. The outer work involves building a more regenerative world. I will direct you to a number of resources in terms of where to shop, what to buy, and how to plant a garden, support farmers, compost, and advocate for regenerative-friendly laws. However, the reality is, at the time of writing this we still don't live in a regenerative world. At the same time, there are a plethora of actions any one of us can take to make a profound difference. They might feel like baby steps, but no matter what you are doing, tell this story and pass it along to your friends and loved ones. We actually get to co-create the new world from all directions.

Without a doubt, we need to heal our institutions, our notion of a healthy economy, and the intergenerational injustices wrought by patriarchy. As we dig in, our relationship to self-care and inner work must remain strong. Just as a well can get dried up, if we take too much from ourselves without giving ourselves time to rest and replenish, we can become martyrs instead of co-creators. Thankfully, we can remember that we are working with nature, Spirit, each other, and the universe. And just as the regenerative agriculture model is all about working with nature and replenishing what we take to create more abundance, we can create regenerative lifestyles that allow us to both give and receive in balance.

WHERE TO START: PUT YOUR BODY ON THE EARTH

Step one: put your body on the earth. Ideally your whole body, belly to the earth, but just finding bare feet or hands on the earth once a day is a start. Placing your hands in the soil to grow living beings or walking and lying on the earth for a period of time are even better. There's a magical area of second growth forest in Oregon I love to visit and in which I hold retreats. When it's warm enough, and even when it's not, I wander around barefoot over the soft, rich soil. My body and entire system calm down in a way that I can't fully explain. It's like a total reset for my nervous system, body, and soul. Sleeping in a small cabin next to a rushing creek in the pitch dark has also afforded me some of the best sleep I've ever had—the darkness and the sound of water simulate the womb, and I feel sure that my body has done some intergenerational mother healing in my sleep there. I've also had incredible sleep in a tent on a beach next to the ocean on Catalina Island—with no electrical lights or road noise, with waves as the only sound and my body only two cloth layers away from soft sand.

In both instances, I slept so long (up to fifteen hours multiple nights in a row) that people were genuinely concerned about me! All this is to say that there are profoundly restorative effects of connecting with the earth directly. For my sense of well-being, connectedness to nature, and health, nothing beats lying on the earth. In grounding, we literally *ground* electrons in our bodies the way we ground wires and electronic devices. Most certainly, when I go too long without touching the earth directly, I can feel it in my body. It makes sense from a practical and physical as well as spiritual and metaphysical perspective—our bodies are part of the Great Mother, materially and energetically. As part of the interconnected web of all things visible and invisible, our bodies are never separated from the soil from which we all come.

Before I do any healing work, I ground and center. To ground, we find our feet on the earth and root into the Mother. To center, we find our central axis and imagine a bright line moving through the center of our body, out through the tops of our heads into the universe, and down to the center of the earth. To me, being grounded also means being grounded in truth, being present on this earth and in my body, and fully acknowledging my birthright to be here and my connection to the earth through my body in physical form on this planet. It means being energetically centered and owning my personal power. Being grounded is the key to abundance and the inflow and outflow of energy. Simply bringing attention to the breath is a path to Spirit, expansiveness, and the cosmos. To remember the truth of my inner, authentic spirit self, literally all I have to do is remember that I'm on the earth and breathing, and notice the spaces between. It transforms automatic forms of consciousness into awareness. Jack Kerouac captures it beautifully:

> Everything is ecstasy, inside. We just don't
> know it because of our thinking-minds.
> But in our true blissful essence of mind is
> known that everything is alright forever
> and forever and forever. Close your eyes,
> let your hands and nerve-ends drop, stop
> breathing for 3 seconds, listen to the silence
> inside the illusion of the world, and you will
> remember the lesson you forgot, which was
> taught in immense milky way soft cloud
> innumerable worlds long ago and not even
> at all. It is all one vast awakened thing. I
> call it the golden eternity. It is perfect.[1]

Nature, life, and our authentic selves are all the same thing, and they're all perfect. To draw life up from the root requires life force energy. Taking the road less traveled will become normal within our lifetimes. As the old status quo cracks and falls away, aligning with nature will become more and more obvious as a path to walk. Our souls are calling and Mother Nature is reminding us. Nature is infinitely abundant. To draw down into the root and manifest also requires life force energy and connectedness. Everything is already perfectly designed to work incredibly well.

We've been messing with this perfect system because we've been blind to the divine. We want something so much better than what we've been doing, and we know it. We're tired of not being able to eat food that is safe and having our lives at odds with what's good for the planet. We're tired of feeling helpless to all of it, and we feel tremendous guilt and shame in knowing that we're part of the problem every day. We don't know how to bring it all together—to find the harmony that our inner knowing is crying out for. But we do know that to bring life is divine. To honor death is divine. We know that we actually live in a world of infinite possibilities. Nature's inherent design is to thrive, to heal, and to create. Look around outside. Nature is designed toward beauty, abundance, harmony, reciprocity, interconnectedness, and utter perfection. We can find both hope and action in the nature within us.

This observation is a prayer, as well as a form of self-care. It's not surprising that we are not taking care of the world very well, given how poorly most of us are taking care of ourselves. This is where self-love comes in, something that most of us struggle with, many of us without even realizing it. The first steps toward healing these wounds involve bringing them into consciousness and starting to understand what's going on. Once we're clear, we can move forward in a positive direction with intention.

CALMING THE NERVOUS SYSTEM

For the body, yin energy is rest-and-receive mode. Most of society has been in hyper-yang mode for millennia. We and the earth are burnt out. Our entire collective is just beginning to understand what it might mean to unwind, to let go, to receive nourishment from the earth without mining, forcing, or taking. The energy of receiving is quite different from taking. The first thing we all get to do is calm our completely fried nervous systems. Here are some of my favorite ways:

► Breathe with intention
► Hum/chant/sing
► Walk
► Dance/jump/shake
► Connect with the outdoors

All of these activities help us get into our bodies, out of our minds, and into a more connected state. When I first started practicing yin yoga, I couldn't get enough of it. I leaned into teaching it, and I'm surprised to this day how resistant people can still be. Even in something as inherently restorative and quieting as yoga, I've witnessed so many people who are crawling out of their skin with discomfort if a yoga class moves too slowly. People wonder if it's worth the money to "not get a workout."

Our ability to let go—even for an hour—to release, breathe slowly, and receive restorative benefits to our bodies, will lead us on a much healthier path, and one that's more aligned with nature. Our inner voice can only emerge when we quiet down and begin to move slowly and gently. To even begin to face the magnitude of the climate emergency, we must tune in to self-care. As much as this moment may seem like a fight for our lives, the way is through the yin—through rooting down, receiving, and connecting with the divine intelligence that is guiding us.

The breath is our connection to Spirit—our path and constant, built-in reminder. Intentionally slowing the breath automatically calms the nervous system. Any time we feel wound up or out of sync, we can remember to breathe. Even just a few intentional breaths can have a healing and recentering effect. Sound is also incredibly healing. We all know the pure joy we can experience by singing along with our favorite song as loud as we want. The vibration of our own voice can heal, align, re-center, and calm our entire system. Sound healing can have profound effects on the body, mind, and spirit.

Similarly, simple walking or any kind of gentle movement outdoors is incredibly nourishing. The recent popularity of forest bathing highlights how this ancient, simple practice can strengthen our immune systems and boost our moods.[2] It can be easy to forget to move our bodies and get outside. Breathing some fresh air while moving can be a profound healing balm, and any sort of ecstatic dance, jumping, and shaking can help us release embodied trauma.

My first therapist also introduced me to *Waking the Tiger: Healing Trauma*, which opened my eyes to the incredible healing power of shaking and movement. In it, Peter Levine and Ann Frederick describe how animals freeze in near-death situations, and when they survive, they literally shake it off. We all encounter multiple traumatic events throughout our lives, even things like a near-miss while driving a car. We can clear out our systems on a regular basis by being in communication with our bodies, feeling in, and shaking things off the way animals do in nature.[3] Being in tune with our somatic nervous system can help us find a sense of peace and relaxation in our lives. When we find our relax and receive mode (the yin), our bodies and minds are far more open to everything, including our inner truth. From that place, we can explore more layers of the energetic mapping of the human body and how they relate to our outer experience.

As much as possible, tune in to your sensory world. How visually peaceful and harmonious is your environment? How is your audioscape? What is the ratio of electronic and mechanical noise to silence and the sounds of the outdoors and music? Notice your smellscape, too. Have you tried fresh herbs, fruits, flowers, and essential oils for aromatherapy? Do you have access to fresh air? How are the taste sensations in your world? How clean is your water and how delicious is the food you eat? And how does your world physically feel? Are you using natural or synthetic fibers in your home, and are you honoring the physical elements in your life? By sticking with natural light (sunlight and fire light), natural sounds (crickets and bodies of water), natural smells (fresh plants and essential oils), natural fibers, and rich, natural tastes, you can vastly improve the quality of your life and calm your nervous system. Turning electronics and Wi-Fi off, going into airplane mode, and unplugging devices entirely can also provide the calm you need for sleep and rest.

SOUL SOIL EXERCISES

► Lay on your back and breathe normally for at least five minutes without interruption (if possible, make yourself super comfortable with a pillow, blanket, soothing music, aromatherapy, etc.). Then take out your journal and freewrite for at least five minutes about what came up for you. How did it feel to lay down and simply breathe? If you felt resistance, what came up for you? If you felt nourished, what did you learn? Can you incorporate this into part of your daily routine? Try this both indoors and outdoors.

► Jump, dance, or shake for the length of your favorite song. How does your body feel afterwards? Is any stress or tension released? Describe the state of your nervous system and any thoughts running through your mind before and after.

► Assess your sensory world. Wherever possible take away electronic noise, car noise, artificial light, and Wi-Fi . . . even for a few minutes a day. Replace these with sounds and smells of nature, essential oils, sun, candles and fire light, natural fibers, and nourishing foods. Do this for a week and freewrite in your journal for at least five minutes a day about the changes you're making and how they feel.

7

RETURNING TO
OUR ROOTS

Both my yoga practice and my work on soil health brought me to my root chakra. Every thread I follow continues to bring me to the same place—home, within myself, into my body, to Mother Nature. Through the process of reconnecting with soil, I have found my innate worthiness. Root chakra work is about our foundations, home, family, safety, value, and nourishment, and is the key to healing from the ground up. Much of the work we'll be discussing in this chapter has to do with healing parts of our root chakra.

As our systems and external reality shift and transform, we are finding our way home. To do our good work in the world, we must understand that we belong here. That our value is inherent as a living part of the universe. That we don't have to earn our value outside of ourselves. We have been running on fear only because we have forgotten who we are. When we take back our power, we take back the narrative and change the game for humanity. If our money or house suddenly disappear, who are we? If our social status suddenly shifts, or a relationship or job ends, who are we? What are we staking our identity and worthiness in?

In remembering who we are and our place in the universe, we remember that our power, our value, our worthiness is our birthright. By incarnating, like every other entity, we are born whole. The creative life force of the universe flows through us and every other part of the universe. Death is simply transformation, a changing of forms. As we remember this simple truth, humanity is passing through a collective death and rebirth. The way forward is to remember who we are and step back into our power as sovereign beings. The systems of destruction don't stand a chance against the internal light, love, and life force within each of us.

This may feel hard to imagine when we feel our sense of worthiness kicked by something external: a breakup, losing a job, a diminished bank account, any sense of personal embarrassment or perceived failure, or—let's say—a pandemic that shuts the whole world down. I promise, all of these are illusions at the soul level. I know they feel quite real in the moment, where ego has us in its grips of fear, but even in the darkest of situations we can drop all the way in and remember the truth of who we are. No matter how disoriented we feel, this step literally requires us to find our feet, touch the earth, and imagine rooting down. Our imaginations are powerful engines for co-creating our reality.

BASIC INTRODUCTION TO THE CHAKRA SYSTEM

I knew nothing of the chakra system when I went to Bali for yoga teacher and craniosacral therapy training. I couldn't wrap my practical and academically trained mind around the idea of energetic spinning discs that somehow related to aspects of myself and my life, and I had even less of an idea of how to heal or align such things to improve my well-being. Now I use the chakra system as a simple and core foundation of checking in with my internal sense of balance and overall wellness. Interestingly enough, the chakra system has parallels in several different traditions, including Maslow's hierarchy of needs in the Western psychology paradigm.

Eastern Body, Western Mind: Psychology and the Chakra System as a Path to the Self remains one of the foundational books of my life. I return to Anodea Judith's work again and again, and portions of it take on entirely new life as my journey unfolds. I honestly have no idea how I understood life before working with the chakra system, and I'm still learning.

Think of the chakra system as an energetic map. We are born with this map in our bodies, and it tells the story of how aligned and in tune we are with the earth and the cosmos. To review, the basic chakra system (from the Hindu tantric traditions) consists of the root, sacral, solar plexus, heart, throat, third eye, and crown chakras.

▶ The root chakra (Muladhara) sits at the base of the chakra system, below the base of your spine. It represents safety and security, as well physical structure, nourishment, and having basic needs met. It is associated with the earth element, masculine energy, and the color red.

▶ The second is our sacral chakra (Svadhisthana), which sits below the navel and stands for creativity, sexuality (reproductive or unconscious creativity), sensuality, relationship, and the emotional body. It embodies the water element and feminine energy, and is associated with the color orange.

▶ The third chakra is the solar plexus (Manipura) which sits below the center of the ribcage. It represents will, self-esteem, confidence, personal power, and the authentic self. It corresponds with the fire element and masculine energy, and is associated with the color yellow.

▶ The fourth chakra is the heart chakra (Anahata), which represents love, emotion, grief, compassion, and joy. It's associated with the air element, feminine energy, and the color green.

▸ The fifth chakra is the throat chakra (Visuddha), which represents truth, speaking our truth, and manifestation through vibration (conscious creativity). It embodies the element of ether and masculine energy, and is associated with the color blue.

▸ The sixth chakra is the third eye (Ajna), just above and in between the eyebrows. It stands for intuition, clear seeing, and imagination. It represents light, inner sounds, and feminine energy, and is associated with the color purple.

▸ The seventh chakra is the crown (Sahasrara), which sits atop the head as a thousand-petaled crown. It represents our connection to divinity, the higher self, the universe, and universal intelligence and energy. This chakra embodies the element of pure light and is associated with bright white, golden, and violet light.

As I stated, the chakra system is like a map—an archetypal and alchemical energetic map within our bodies. The heart is where the upper three and lower three chakras meet, bridging heaven and earth along a rainbow. Most people in Western society are unfortunately disconnected from the bottom three chakras, which leaves us feeling profoundly ungrounded and insecure. Fear-based culture has been both the cause and effect of this disjuncture and disconnection from our roots, from within ourselves, and from the Great Mother.

Through this lens, perhaps we can see just how important our human connection to the earth is in terms of our personal well-being. The energetic home, root, and starting place of our systems are the basis of how we feel and how well we operate in the world. Most of us frankly feel terrified, insecure, stuck in comparison, exhausted, overwhelmed, and completely confused as to how to make things any better. Most of us turn to

Eastern or ancient healing modalities when we are at an absolute breaking point, or when Western medicine runs out of answers for us. The reality is there aren't enough pill-based medications in the world to handle what ails us. From our personal health to climate change, for quite some time we have been treating symptoms instead of systems. We have been collectively blind to the root problem within us, in front of us, and directly beneath our feet.

At the most fundamental level, we feel like we don't belong. We don't know what the hell we are doing here, and we are terrified. We feel like we need to earn our place in a universe that in actuality has chosen us, loves us, and co-created us with a perfectly intact map of itself inside of us. Getting grounded means remembering who we are and what we are doing here. Getting oriented. It means connecting with our inherent safety and security in this world. It means connecting with our most innate knowing, the ancestral depth and love within us. Remembering our place in the grand dance of all things—the forests, the oceans, the deserts, the flowers, and the bees. It means remembering the Great Mother's eternal love. It means remembering the protective structure of the divine masculine within us. Humanity's life on earth depends on this remembering. Take a deep breath. Begin to remember.

> The real magic is that to keep the system in equilibrium, the plant also gives back to the system and the whole cycle goes round and round. Nature works in balance, sustainability, and regeneration through the give-and-receive exchange of all things.

Reconnecting to and rebalancing our root chakra helps us retrieve our souls. As we call our power back from external institutions, we can work with our nervous systems to heal current and past traumas. Similar to the trauma freeze response discussed in the last section, when we undergo experiences in our lives that we don't have tools for, we tend to exile entire parts of ourselves until we feel rooted and calm enough to receive them. When our energetic system is working properly, we feel inherently safe in ourselves and can fully feel and release experiences in real time. An aligned energetic system feels strong, safely held, and flowing with ease. If we are unprepared for certain experiences, our system puts them away somewhere in our psyche, in our body, and in our field until we are ready.

Doing our inner work in these times means strengthening and clearing our systems to the point where we can revisit our more difficult experiences and reintegrate them. The world is currently in the process of a massive root chakra healing, purging, and clearing. Old belief systems about safety and security—particularly with regard to placing our power outside of ourselves in external institutions—are falling apart at every level. Getting grounded involves facing into this process, being present with it, and feeling through it—at the personal and collective levels.

SOUL SOIL EXERCISES

▶ Find a quiet space to sit and breathe, ideally outdoors (but indoors will also work). If possible, lay on your belly on the earth. Imagine roots unfurling from the base of your spine and any part of you that is touching the ground and into dark, rich soil (even if you are inside). Now scan your body for anything that does not serve and imagine it dropping out through the roots into the earth. When you are ready, imagine yourself drawing nourishment up from the earth, through your roots, and into your body. Be with this sensation and breathe normally for as long as feels good.

► Next, take out your journal and freewrite for at least ten minutes about your relationship with your roots, family, identity, tribe, and sense of being supported and safe. Notice what comes up and start to feel into any places that may be calling for attention and healing. Note any thought forms that come up that feel particularly prickly or difficult (we can use these in the next section).

► Feel yourself fully supported by the earth, either sitting, standing, or lying down. Feel Mother Earth supporting your full weight and relax completely into her. Notice the sense of being completely held. Stay here for as long as feels good.

8

WE ARE INHERENTLY WORTHY

Because the root chakra represents our "roots" into the soil—our connection to the Great Mother—it has everything to do with our sense of security and safety. The earth literally supports our bodies: all of our food, water, and shelter comes from Great Mother Earth. Often when we feel insecure and afraid, we have an imbalance in our root chakra. Our root connects us to nourishment and being held, which helps us understand our inherent worthiness. With a healthy root, we know we belong.

Our time in the womb and as a baby also informs the development of our root chakra. Mindset and inner child work are critical in this process of healing from the ground up, where we hold our inner child safe as our higher self, communicate with it, and essentially re-parent ourselves as integrated adults, welcoming exiled parts of ourselves back. We can remind these parts of ourselves that even though we didn't know it at the time, we are infinitely safe, loved, secure, and welcome, and that we belong in this benevolent universe. Like remembering and integrating the Great Mother and the forgotten goddess archetypes, we can remember and integrate fragmented and forgotten parts of ourselves.

Holding our inner child can be quite simple. In any moment of contraction, we can sit with the child version of ourselves, hold that child as our higher self, and ask what it has to say. When we can tune in and feel in, often we'll hear the voice of the inner child say something like "I'm not good enough." And we can actually feel the feelings that we felt as that child in real time. From here, we can utilize tools like Byron Katie's *The Work* (some of the most life-changing work I've ever done) to inquire with the thought forms that come up. The reality is that our thoughts run our emotions, and there's a direct line between what our brains think and what we feel in our bodies. Until we can separate the two, we are inevitably run by our thought forms, but once we can identify and question them, we can forgive ourselves for believing any misunderstandings about being anything other than whole and perfect in every moment. We can then integrate new thoughts and consciously shift our outdated patterns.

Our thoughts do not define us. Our conditioning does not define us. The sooner we can untether ourselves from the prison inside our own minds, the sooner we can unleash our truest love and expression into the world. Feeling like we're going to die at every soul-expanding juncture is a universal tell. That unmistakable shaking, sweating, and desire to run away is the key. We are not our thoughts. We are not our conditioning. We have a choice in every moment. And in every moment we can choose Spirit and choose to remember. This is the path to empowerment. To untangle ourselves from conditioned stories is the way.

I received the following gift of self-forgiveness practice from one of my coaches, Alyssa Nobriga. Once you have identified and inquired around a particular thought form, say the following:

> I forgive myself for believing in the
> misunderstanding that [original thought
> form]. The truth is [whatever is true for you].[1]

This generally sounds something like, "I forgive myself for believing in the misunderstanding that I'm not good enough. The truth is I am infinitely worthy. The truth is I am a drop of the universe. The truth is I am power, light, and love." In *The Gene Keys*, Richard Rudd describes forgiveness as a force that comes in from the future, meets the present, and heals the past.[2] In this sense, forgiveness heals intergenerational lines and dissolves timelines entirely.

Understanding my role in the universe and my inherent worthiness is how I can identify the truth. I came to this knowledge through first becoming aware of the ego and my higher self, learning about the benevolence and aliveness of the universe, starting to interact directly with it through spiritual practice and connection with my higher self, and then beginning to recognize myself as the drop of the infinite universe that I had always intuited myself to be. This unfolding can arrive through a combination of life experience, personal work, studying spiritual teachings, your own intuition and inner knowing, and ceremony. When we sit with these difficult emotions and thought forms, we are able to redirect ourselves back around to the truth. Knowing that I'm a co-creating piece of a benevolent universe is critical to healing these wounds and releasing unhelpful thought forms.

In the process of this work, I've found the places where I've rejected younger, more wounded versions of myself. There have been chapters of my life where I've been unconsciously unkind because I was so afraid and so programmed to try to control others and situations to keep myself safe. I've found places where I've exiled entire versions of myself, and I am working to reintegrate and forgive. At this juncture, when my egoic brain jumps up to protect me by comparing or judging, I can observe it, thank it with love, forgive the thought forms inspiring pain, and carry on as a whole being. But it has taken years to discover and develop these tools within myself, and I haven't had them for most of my life. So my practice is to welcome those parts of myself that didn't yet know the love of the infinite universe. I've cried my eyes out holding parts of myself—parts that felt perpetually unsafe and tried to control external circumstances to create a sense of safety, because they didn't yet remember how safe and loved in the universe I have always been. This practice also helps me hold space for others who are coming from a place of fear and pain.

Self-forgiveness is the path to forgiving others. It's the only way to clear the inner debris of negative self-talk, the inner critic, the comparing mind, and all the other thought forms that can clog the pathway to Spirit, which is our birthright. We all have it in us. Even those of us who have done years of work. Both the challenge and the opportunity lie here. Self-forgiveness is the path to inner peace.

> To bring Muladhara to consciousness is to
> bring awareness to our roots, to uncover
> the past, to examine it, to delve into it.
> Everything that grows above branches
> out into infinity, growing more complex.
> Going down to our roots brings us into
> a singular simplicity, and anchors us
> into the commonality of the collective
> unconscious. It brings us home to earth.[3]
>
> ANODEA JUDITH

Collectively, we are revisiting and reintegrating the wounds of our experiences over lifetimes spanning the last five to ten thousand years. Certainly, the lasting wounds of patriarchy of the last three thousand years (at least) require the most compassionate and humble reintegration. The grief and rage from thousands of years of atrocities and disconnection from ourselves, each other, and the Mother are all too real. We get to feel through all of these emotions, while holding ourselves safe with our remembrance of universal love and the interconnectedness of all things.

The truth is the North Star to which we can all align. We get to ask ourselves collectively what our truth is and choose how the story ends. The truth might not be pretty, or well packaged, or at all what we expect. But in every cell of our bodies there is an ancient knowing. We know the truth. We know that the design of all things is inherently perfect and interconnected. We can see how seemingly much larger cycles (like the carbon and water cycles) are tied directly into the life cycles of the small (or what we think of as the small). We can even see that small and large are one, if we only shift and widen our perspective.

We are inextricably embodied and interconnected. Food and breath are the two constant embedded reminders that we are intimately interconnected with everything around us—in perfect balance, intake, and release. There is no such thing as waste. Everything is perfectly designed to cycle back into abundance. Again, the words *human* and *humility* derive from the Latin *humus* and the Greek *hamai*, which both mean "earth" or "ground." As we rework our world and save ourselves, it will be born from humility rather than hubris. The solution to our most confronting problems is here and always has been. Nature is not shy about revealing her secrets. We just have to listen.

SOUL SOIL EXERCISES

► Spend a day noticing every time an unpleasant feeling comes up. Carry a small journal with you or make a quick note in your phone about the feeling and some of the surrounding circumstances.

► At the end of the day, pick one of the experiences that you noted and practice sitting with your inner child. Imagine yourself as your higher self, and tune in to the presence of the inner child. When you get there, ask the inner child what it has to say. Journal about its response until you can distill some clear thought forms like "I'll be rejected" or "I'm not good enough." Hold your inner child safe as your higher self.

▶ When you feel ready and open, sit with the thought and inquire about whether or not it's true (a la Byron Katie's *The Work*). When complete, try some of the self-forgiveness suggestions mentioned above.

9

REMEMBERING WE
ARE NATURE:
GROWING OUR OWN FOOD

Another immediate way to begin root chakra healing—and both inner and outer work in general—is to grow our own food and compost. It's also an incredibly practical and cost-effective activity in uncertain times. In fact, growing our own food and reconnecting with Mother Nature is an act of revolution. In a world in which the systems that have brought us to where we currently are have proven inadequate, having a direct connection to the earth herself along with the ability to feed ourselves is the ultimate root chakra safety. It helps us with physical, nutritional, financial, psychological, and spiritual autonomy.

Growing our own food redirects our power back into our own field, pulls it away from highly destructive industrial agricultural systems, and counteracts the devastating effects of deforestation. Saving our seeds is a human right, and one that takes our power back from those who would try to patent nature. It's also something we can do every day for free. The current systems only stand if we continue to participate in them. At the end of the day, our food, our homes, and our bodies all come from Mother Earth, and we can realign ourselves with her.

Growing our own food can mean a tiny pot inside an apartment, a raised bed in the backyard, or a more developed garden if we have the space. The easiest first step is to begin to grow things that come from food scraps—carrot tops, beet tops, and lettuce all regrow themselves in just half an inch of water. All it takes is placing the pieces you cut off and putting them in water in a window container—shallow plastic take-out food containers work great, and including them in your food production means reusing plastic. Garlic chives will also sprout from an individual clove, and onion chives will sprout from an onion end. Additionally, you can save all manner of vegetable scraps in the freezer and use them for vegetable broth before they're composted.

Imagine how much free value (along with considerably less food waste) these few steps can afford. Seeds can be harvested for free directly from food you've already purchased (for example, tomato and pepper seeds). And like I suggested above, you can repurpose all manner of plastic containers (and cardboard, including boxes) for planters. The only thing you need to purchase is potting soil. Also, if you have the space, making your own compost is fairly easy. Most people don't realize how much more connected and aligned with Mother Nature we can be (and for free) in just a few simple steps.

Robin Wall Kimmerer, a member of the Citizen Potawatomi Nation and a botanist, writes about how we can love a garden and it can love us back in her path-opening *Braiding Sweetgrass: Indigenous Wisdom, Scientific Knowledge, and the Teachings of Plants*. I experience my garden very much that way. The joy of cultivating and tending to little plants, interacting with them and the soil, taking only what I need for food, and thanking them is part of every meal. Imagine honoring the earth, our food, our bodies, and our spirits through love and care this way.

And if you feel like you want some extra guidance before beginning, stop by your nearest nursery or talk to a friend who gardens in the area. Get the scoop about your local plants and soil, as every area is different. Start to ask for advice, and then just dive in! Buy some organic soil, set up whatever sized garden you have the space for, or participate in your local community garden. Pick some easy plants to start with (I recommend herbs or cherry tomatoes) and start experimenting! Plant what you love and keep sharing information with others. Before long you'll be learning about saving seeds, how different plants respond to variations in light and moisture, and how to take the seasons into account. Over time, you'll gather all the information you need to keep moving forward. If some plants die along the way, thank them, respectfully compost them, and keep trying. You actually can't do it wrong. You might even end up howling at the moon.

For most seeds and roots, repopulating mycorrhizal fungi is also relatively easy and affordable. It can be purchased inexpensively as a soil amendment, and can even be purchased online. So the first step is to stop using pesticides and herbicides that kill microbial life and make plants sick, and then to apply compost and soil amendments to repopulate life in the soil. We can also stop using industrial chemicals on our lawns, instead opting for local and drought-resistant plants. We also keep the soil covered with cover crops and compost rather than turning it or tilling it, which unfortunately exposes the microbes to soil and sometimes breaks the tender web of mycorrhizal fungi. By protecting and amending the soil with compost and microbes, we nourish the soil and the plants to the point that they can once again draw carbon into the soil. The healthier the soil and plant life, the more carbon we can sequester from the atmosphere.

Regenerating soil is by far the cheapest (and most doable) way to sequester carbon, especially compared to the billions we have already spent on research involving the carbon sequestration technology still under development. Repopulating soil life is a no-brainer. Take simple steps to plant food and drought-resistant plants with healthy soil, and partake in the joy, security, health, and autonomy of saving your seeds.

Living a regenerative life is all about the sacred connection of all life. We are physically made of the same stuff everything else is, and we are in symbiosis with everything that lives, as well. Healing the soil is inherently divine work. With each inhale and exhale we are in constant exchange with nature—we literally exchange elements (including carbon and oxygen) with the plants around us. There is no separation. We forget that all life is cyclical, not linear. To draw life up from the root requires life force energy. When we realize that all things move in cycles, we no longer have to fear the darkness, or the night, or death.

My force-of-nature teacher in Bali, Cat Kabira, dropped this gem in a class: "As we are returning to our own true nature, we remember we are part of nature." I scribbled it down, and with every breath, I started to get it. With every conscious breath, we are exchanging with all that is—living and dying. This is why even gentle yoga and breathwork are so powerful. The breath fuels every truth we speak and every song we sing. The breath is our path, our constant reminder of the divine within us. Food is the other divine reminder of cycles: what we take in from the earth becomes our bodies, and what we let go of goes back to fertilize and bring forth new life. In this way, we all have built-in, constant reminders of the life-death-life cycles, and yet we still manage to constantly forget the truth of cycles and interconnection. Everything is one. It's actually the most simple and obvious truth, but it comes forth only when we quiet down enough to listen. The earth is telling us, our bodies are telling us, and life itself is reminding us with each breath—our true nature. By losing sight of our own truth, we've lost sight of larger truths, and the consequences are painfully evident.

Our healthy relationship with the earth is not a given. Like tending a fire or tending the soil, it requires awareness, presence, and care. As someone who once had to move eight times in the course of three years, I can personally speak to the importance of home, security, and safety. Most of us in the West tend to take having a place to call home for granted. But I've come to learn, and painfully, that home is not a given. It must be cultivated, created, and protected. Our inner worlds and our outer worlds must be cared for and nourished, and only then can they care for and nourish us. Once again, we find ourselves back to building our bridge from here to there with attention to detail, diligence, and patience.

FOOD AND NUTRIENTS

Flavor is a telling indicator of the nutrient richness in food. Not all vegetables are created equal. If you've ever eaten tomato grown in rich healthy soil or tasted a wild strawberry, you know what I mean. That pop of incredible flavor is nature's message to our bodies that the food is nutrient rich and good to eat. Conversely, if you've eaten a tomato from a fast food joint or supermarket that tastes like cardboard, you also know what I mean.

The amount of nutrients in American fruits and vegetables has vastly declined over the last sixty years, since the mass spread of industrial agriculture. The amount of vitamin C in an American orange is forty percent less than it was sixty years ago. If you never buy straight from local farms, or grow your own organic food, or travel to Europe, there's a decent chance that you have no idea what a truly nutritious orange actually tastes like. That bland excuse of an orange that you are now eating is in fact mostly sugar. That's right, your salad is quickly turning into a pile of soggy carbs. Delicious.

Also, if it's not organic, your salad was also covered with a blanket of insecticides and herbicides at some point. As it turns out, a healthy plant does not need any of that toxic intervention, and what we think of as pests are usually a sign of disease and illness. Back to the cycles of things, pests are, for the most part, there to clean out the plants that aren't doing so well. If our plants are drawing pests or an invasive fungus, it probably means the plant is not getting what it needs from the soil.

Here's a different type of cycle for you: We kill the microbial life in the soil and thereby undermine the plant's ability to get the nutrients it needs. Then the plant attracts pests. To fight the pests, we spray the plant with pesticides and herbicides, which, in turn, kill more microbial life. On top of that, because we've disrupted the nutrient cycle, we add chemical fertilizers to put back the stuff that would be naturally present if only we hadn't killed off our microbial friends in the first place. Honestly, it's utter insanity.

Plants communicate with each other through the underground network of fungi and other microbes. They send signals to each other and release chemicals that indicate what is going on with them. I recommend *The Hidden Life of Trees: What They Feel, How They Communicate—Discoveries from a Secret World* by Peter Wohlleben and *Fantastic Fungi: How Mushrooms Can Heal, Shift Consciousness, and Save the Planet* by Paul Stamets and others for a thorough look at what goes on beneath our feet. When a plant is attacked by some sort of intruder, for example, it sends signals to the other plants in the system, which are then able to release chemicals to protect themselves. Plants have even been known to share their nutrients underground with other plants who are not getting enough sunlight because they are in the shade. Beautiful, profound, and totally on point. All of life is one, we are in constant exchange, and within us lies that inner knowing.

Here again, the spiritual meets the practical. Food grown in poor soil that has been sprayed with pesticides or herbicides is essentially sickly and devoid of what it needs, even if it makes it to our dinner table. Yuck. And the most insane part of it all is that we are undermining a system that was already designed to work! For millions of years, humanoids and plants and microbes and animals have co-evolved to work out a system that benefits everyone, and instead of working with that system (like the chef in Italy I'll tell you about in a bit), we decided that we could do better by taking out parts of the system and replacing them. As a result, tomatoes taste like wet paper and our food in general—what is supposed to be our holy nourishment—makes us sick over time. The only people this broken system benefits are the owners of and investors in corporations who make pesticides, fertilizers, and pharmaceuticals. All the while, we're getting sicker by the day and spending billions of dollars trying to figure out why.

Shitty food, by the way, affects a lot more than our health and the size of our bellies and butts. It has everything to do with how we feel and how we *be* in the world. Even when we eat vegetables (which we typically associate with being a healthy choice), more often than not we are ingesting deprived food from a depraved source. Given that we are in constant exchange of our food, it should come as no surprise that what we eat affects everything in our bodies, including the microbes in our guts, which help us do what we need to do. We're still learning how eating fermented foods and other probiotics help us repopulate the microbes in our guts that we've killed off by using antibiotics. The soil microbiome is most likely the gut microbiome's nerdy cousin.

Research is pouring out all over the place that links our mistreatment of gut microbes to physical ailments such as autoimmune disorders, as well as problems with our moods and emotional states.[1] The medical establishment, which has always viewed soil microbes as distinct from those that live in our guts, is starting to realize that the two types aren't so disconnected after all. We've already known that there are microbes in the soil that act as antidepressants when we touch them—yet another reason to garden and interact with the soil with our hands.

In some basic sense, soil is life and we are soil. What we put in our bodies matters, well beyond the physical. Without a doubt, we can do a whole lot better than we are right now. We just have to keep in mind how all of these interrelated parts play together, and understand what that means for all of us. Ultimately we'll know by the food we grow.

SOUL SOIL EXERCISES

▶ When you purchase your food for the week, buy at least one thing that you can eat and regrow (I recommend carrots, beets, lettuce, garlic, or onions for beginners). If it's at all possible to purchase organic and from a farmer's market, do so. For tops and lettuce bottoms, find a container in your home that you can fill with half an inch of water and place the remainder of your chosen vegetable in the water near a window. If you are an advanced practitioner already, share this exercise with a friend and help them learn. Notice how it feels to regenerate your own food.

▶ Harvest seeds from something you can regrow. I recommend tomato, bell pepper, or jalapeño seeds for beginners, from which you can simply remove the seeds directly, dry them on a paper towel, and store them in a bag, plastic container, or jar. You can also go on YouTube and watch a short video about how to harvest seeds from your chosen food. When you're ready, plant as many seeds as you like in a little bit of potting soil. Save the rest in a baggie or reusable container. Notice how it feels to interact with soil and harvest seeds for free. If you've done this type of thing for a while, share it with someone else and encourage them along the way. How does it feel to remember that your food is a living being?

▶ At the end of the week, take out your journal and freewrite for at least ten minutes about your experiences with seeds. How did it feel to work with nature to create your own food for free? Check in once you get some sprouts and journal for another ten minutes about the process. What feelings do the new sprouts elicit?

10

FACING DEATH AND REGENERATION: COMPOST AND HEALING WITH INDIGENOUS PEOPLES AND LANDS

The flip side of growing food is composting. If sprouts are new life, compost is the death aspect of the cycle. Food waste can actually serve as nutrients for the soil and feed the next round of sprouts. Composting is a form of giving back to Mother Nature and the cycles of nourishment, and it's also a reminder that the things we think we can't use can actually be returned to the earth with care and used for something else (the material version of releasing any energy from our bodies that doesn't serve us).

Composting also heals and protects microbial life. This means taking your organic waste (fruit and vegetable cuttings, as well as yard clippings) and allowing it to decompose and become fertilizer for plants. At home, you can store organic food scraps in the freezer until your container is full and you need to transport the scraps to your nearest compost option—maybe a green bin at home that your city takes to municipal compost, a box in your backyard, or a neighborhood pile or drop-off location.

If you want to learn about composting, talk to someone who is already doing it. If you don't know anyone who is, get together with some friends and figure it out. Have your children help out, and find out what's happening in your neighborhood and community at large. Spread the word about why composting is so important, and educate yourself about what's happening with local policy.

Compost is a funny thing. I find that it freaks most Americans out. For Europeans and people in other parts of the world, compost is built into their urban systems as a way of life and incorporated into personal gardens. Americans tend to associate compost with trash, bugs, odors, and possibly poop.

Most of us in the US throw away our food and yard waste into the trash. From there, it travels to a landfill with all sorts of other waste (much of which should be recycled, but that's an entirely different book), and because it's not being handled properly, the whole mess emits methane and CO_2 while it's rotting, which only adds to the problem of climate disruption. It's insanity. Let me be clear: food is not trash. Ever. Organic matter is an asset. Check out the incredible work of Pashon Murray and Detroit Dirt. The earth's systems are straight up designed to move everything through a closed-loop, endless, wasteless system. Our entire concept of waste is, in fact, nonsense.

Given what we know about what the patriarchy did to the dark goddess, it's not surprising that we are so out of tune with compost and the natural decay of organic matter. We are terrified of death. To be okay with it, we have to understand that when a life-form dies, it doesn't just disappear into some anesthetized other realm. It decomposes and feeds back into the material system on this earth. Of course, this is true of our bodies and those of our loved ones, and this tends to freak us out, but our human bodies are made of organic material, whether we like it or not. As far as American culture goes, we're pretty into spring and summer, babies being born, and youth culture and so on, but when it comes to darkness, introversion, winter, bugs, poop, and anything that happens underground, we cringe or avert our eyes. Our experience of a worldwide pandemic has profoundly brought this fact to the fore.

To be whole, we must embrace both yin and yang; and to move with the cycles of a healthy earth, we must breathe with it. Death is humbling, and frankly we could use quite a bit of humility right now. It's time to stop fighting what we've always known. All that goes to say that poop is not our enemy, and that we should not throw our food scraps in the trash, but rather compost them. The notion of infinite growth in a finite system is an inherent fail. When we remember how cycles work, we remember that compost also facilitates life. Good compost is teeming with life, and all the critters that help decomposition along are drawn to the compost heap. Composting helps build humus—the healthy, nutrient-dense layer of topsoil that keeps plant life and biodiversity thriving, especially microbial life. A plant supported by a healthy soil ecosystem and a balanced surrounding ecosystem will actually have everything it needs to fight off pests.

In 2013, when I was just starting to learn about soil, I found myself in an incredible garden on the Amalfi coast in Italy. It was attached to a four-star hotel owned by a friend's family (one of the more spoiled moments of my life). During a tour with the hotel's chef, I asked him what he puts on his plants to keep the bugs away. At first, he didn't understand the question. I referred to sprays and pesticides, and he shook his head and said, "Oh! Nothing! We use compost!" Makes sense to me: southern Italy has some of the best soil in the world and, in turn, some of the best water. They've passed the knowledge of how to take care of the soil down through generations, and they've never stopped doing it right. If you've ever had a meal in southern Italy, much of the glory of their incredible food has to do with the soil and water from which it comes.

In the same way that far too many of us treat our bodies, and in the same way that our larger economy affects our bodies, we mine the soil of nutrients without replacing them. Instead of supplementing our bodies and the soil with synthetic replacements, we can approach the whole issue and give back in a healthier way. For our bodies, that means nourishment, rest, slowing down, and connecting with the earth. For our soil, that means composting and making sure the soil becomes rich with life and dark with carbon.

HEALING WITH THE EARTH: INDIGENOUS PEOPLES AND LANDS

When we develop the tools for healing and thereby heal our connection with the land, the land herself starts to share her stories; Mother Nature herself will share her song. For as long as humans have been on the earth, indigenous peoples have nurtured this relationship with the earth and held ancient wisdom for all of time. They have also been severely punished for it.

Beginning to heal the harm that has been done to indigenous peoples and their ways of knowing is intrinsic to healing our relationship with the earth. This conversation is highly sensitive and requires the utmost reverence, as it is tragically fraught with extensive violence and trauma. For nonindigenous peoples, the best place to start is looking within ourselves, at our family history, and the history of the lands we live on, and to begin with questions and an open mind and heart.

Perhaps a more loving relationship among humans, plants, animals, food, water, and land can be restored by honoring indigenous communities and their needs, the land that bears the wounds of genocide, and the wisdom that has been carried and protected by indigenous peoples all over the world. The legacy of the MMIW epidemic (missing and murdered indigenous women and girls) is among the most tragic wounds that we collectively carry, and it requires that we awaken to the continued violence and move to end it. The horrific legacy of residential schools in Canada and the United States is also very much alive to this day (the last one in the US didn't close until 1996).

An exact way forward is unclear. However, it's obvious that we're called to honor and revere what has been harmed. All of our societies and bodies bear the cultural, psychological, and energetic scars of this terrible chapter in our collective past and present. Some initial steps include the following:

► Learn the indigenous history and name of the land you live on, as well as the place where your grandmothers were born. What happened to the indigenous people who lived there?

► Start relationships and honor them. Befriend an indigenous person or organization and ask how you can best help or serve.

► Learn the history of reconciliation in the region and understand what reconciliation means to the indigenous population.

► Learn about how indigenous people from your region treated the land, what was grown and eaten, and how the land was tended.

► Understand the impact colonialism had (and continues to have) on the lives of indigenous people, and commit to taking steps to counter the harm.

► Discover where nonindigenous people support inequality directly or indirectly and find out what can be done to change this.

► Recognize that nonindigenous people personally are not to blame. That being said, also recognize that nonindigenous people are responsible.

- Understand one's own ancestral wounds and connection to the land.

- Realize that much cannot be understood or experienced outside of ceremony.

- Understand the United Nations Declaration on the Rights of Indigenous Peoples (UNDRIP) and First Nations principles of OCAP® (ownership, control, access, and possession), and why they are in place.

- Know about key issues (for example, the MMIW and residential schooling mentioned above).

- Improve your education by taking a course (check out ictinc.ca for options).

Actions like these can help us become aware of our painful shared reality. They can also bring to the fore the beauty of what indigenous peoples have to share and open a door for our collective healing process. Education and relationships are the keys to a way forward. Even bringing this awareness up to bear witness is a starting point, as well as a place from which to finally stop the violence still being enacted today. Perhaps here the gifts of sacred ceremony and protecting lands and waters from destruction can become woven into our hearts and societies. As we know, we are all profoundly interconnected. Harm to one is harm to all, and harm to the earth is harm to us all.

SOUL SOIL EXERCISES

- If you are not already composting, figure out the best way to compost where you are.

If you don't have a municipal green bin or space outdoors, this means researching to find a local drop-off point. Try composting for a week! If you are already an advanced practitioner, find someone to help with their first week of composting. At the end of the week, freewrite about your experience composting for at least ten minutes. How did you feel about contributing less to landfills and giving back to Mother Earth? Are there any challenges that you have run into that can be overcome?

▶ Next find a quiet place and meditate for five to ten minutes on the death part of the life-death-rebirth cycle. Meditate on winter, emptying, the new moon, and compost. Simply breathe normally and allow this reflection to take you wherever it does. If you feel inspired to journal, include any resistance that may have arisen.

▶ Research the land where you live, as well as the land one of your grandmothers was born on, to find out what indigenous peoples lived there. Research the history of colonialism in these areas. Freewrite for at least five minutes about what you've found and what feelings come up. Follow your intuition about what further steps to take in the list above to authentically connect with and heal with indigenous peoples and lands.

PART FOUR

INTEGRATION: DIVINE FEMININE AND DIVINE MASCULINE

All of nature is in divine harmony
in a grand dance between feminine
and masculine energies.

11

LIVING A REGENERATIVE LIFE

The entire universe is the cosmic dance between feminine and masculine energies, and this dance plays out in each of us. Looking within can help us understand where we may have gone out of balance, as well as where we can intentionally bring ourselves back into harmony. Our personal power is most available and alive when we honor this dance, energetic play, and harmony.

A world in which our systems reflect these universal truths and are guided by divine intelligence is possible. It's a world where we are connected through our internal energetic systems and are tuned into our highest selves. Transforming our connection to the soil and healing from the ground up requires us to remember the connection between our bodies, our roots, and all of life.

We have real work to do when it comes to reversing the climate crisis. The first step is to remember who we are and where we came from. As we remember our connection to the soil and our souls, we remember our innate power, and as we do that we can heal our energetic body systems, as well as the systems of the earth. As we remember how to connect to our inner voice and follow divine guidance, we remember that we always have absolutely everything we need. We are a part of a living, co-creative, benevolent universe. We are infinitely worthy, we belong here, and we incarnated to take on this specific task.

Now is the moment to find our feet on the earth, connect to our breath, root down, and rise. We can expand into the possibility before us when we find our roots. The magic of nature is infinite, and as it is, so are we. To find the true magic within us is to integrate the hurts of the past and the present, and to create the peaceful, abundant future we all desire.

Our disconnection from our bodies, from the earth, from the Great Mother and goddess archetypes, is literally killing us. The way home is back into ourselves—into our inner work—that creates our ability to express the outward solutions necessary and co-create together. Finding our sacred sexuality, reconnecting to our true power, maintaining healthy boundaries, and communicating honestly is the way to healing our planet in time.

Humans have always understood our relationship to the Great Mother, but the times we are living in demand that we remember fully and act. The sacred masculine holds the consistent container that allows the sacred feminine to heal and rise again. The sacred masculine also creates the structure that allows the feminine to flow and create life, and the sacred feminine holds the holy vessel that allows the sacred masculine to show up in determined and focused action.

LIVING A REGENERATIVE LIFE: BASIC PRINCIPLES

You now understand quite a bit about the nature of climate change, the Great Mother, and how we became disconnected in such a way as to lose track of the cycles of nature and our bodies. We've learned about our shared wounds and various ways to heal. The stark difference between taking a linear and extractive (mining) approach to life and committing ourselves to more regenerative practices and mindsets is also becoming bountifully clear.

What does it look like to live a regenerative life? One that is not simply sustainable (as in, not poised for inevitable breakdown), but one that actually works with the abundance of nature to create? Step one requires us to set down our armor. That means relinquishing the parts of ourselves that protect the ego with cynicism, judgment, intellectualism, and criticism. These defensive reflexes are merely the actions of a desperate patriarchy and the intergenerational mother and father wounds we all experience, but we can choose differently.

We must not allow our connection to Spirit to be shamed, mocked, or ridiculed; to do so is to propagate the habits of controlling others and ourselves with fear. On the pathway to joy and abundance (and our soul's expression), we often encounter walls of fear. That fear is just the ego's resistance. To the ego, joy feels terrifying.

I offer the following as a gentle review to take step by step. Here are some simple ways to live a regenerative life:

▶ **Sleep.** Get plentiful, restful sleep. Not receiving the gift of this fundamental nourishment is a huge red flag that we are not in alignment. Western culture is famous for sleep-shaming, because it runs against the notion of endless productivity and the habit of mining ourselves in the same way we've mined the earth. Replenishing sleep is an act of revolution. Our wellness is our revolution. We will not get run over by the bullying culture of seriousness that tries to tell us that being run ragged is strong and being well-rested is weak. When our minds spin out so completely that we can't rest well, to the point we need medication in order to sleep at all, something is out of line. That being said, I fully support medication when necessary, especially of the plant medicine variety. I had terrible insomnia as a teenager. I couldn't fall asleep because my mind was incessantly jumping to the next thing I needed to do to achieve, and I was constantly processing personal dramas because I had no inner compass of my own worthiness. Adequate sleep is connected to our breath and our ability to calm our nervous systems and our minds. It's also our connection to the watery, subconscious, underworld dream states, where nature and the goddess speak to us. We must permit ourselves to do "nothing." There's an Italian saying, *Il bel far niente*, which means the "beauty of doing nothing." As it turns out, our systems are actually doing quite a bit while we are doing "nothing." Perhaps it's no mistake that the Roman Empire and Catholic Church staked their ground in southern Italy, some of the most fertile soil on the earth.

► **Food.** Obviously, this book has a lot to do with food. Eating is an act of lovemaking. How many of us have for decades been running around unconsciously or fervently shoving some food-like substance into our faces? Just to get to the next place, to do the next thing? The goddess does not shovel food. Imagine the billions of miraculous interactions in nature that result in the single apple, potato, or leaf of lettuce! The sun shining down with all its infinite love. The poetry and flowing wisdom of the water cycle. How could we believe for a moment that the universe is not benevolent? Like sex, our relationship to food is actually about pleasure, expression, love, and the divine. When we eat, we bow to the Mother. Bury your face in some fertile soil. Be enamored with the garden. Welcome the magic of herbs and flowers. Food is green magic and we are all green witches. We also have a major invitation to get into right relationship with the plant, fungi, and animal kingdoms. Michael Pollan's advice in *In Defense of Food: An Eater's Manifesto* is to "Eat food. Not too much. Mostly plants."[1] That rings true. The industrial agricultural system we have been relying on for decades has been the cause of so much deforestation and soil destruction. Let's learn to take only what we need and to express gratitude for the gifts our Great Mother offers us.

▶ **Movement.** I almost used the word *exercise* here, but *movement* is way better. The body desires to move. Not because we need to be in shape, but because movement is joy. It inspires deeper breaths. It invites us into the moment. I have no idea what the science is behind dance, and I'm not sure there's an explanation. Why in the world do our bodies naturally move to some vibrations? And why does it inspire so much joy when we permit ourselves to let it rip? Why does it hurt so much when we feel suppressed in our movement? Again, feeling our bare feet on the earth is the primordial magic, the sensual language of the goddess.

▶ **Sex.** Amazingly, sex didn't make it to my original list. What? Blind spot. Still, our bodies desire to express themselves, and pleasure is our birthright. When we remember ourselves as part of nature, we remember that sex is so much more than simple procreation. It's artistry. It's dropping all the way in and being present with ourselves and others. This can absolutely mean self-pleasure, sensuality practices, and consensual, enthusiastic sex with whomever. Sex is sacred. One more time: *sex is sacred*. Our creative energy is ours. We belong to ourselves and get to share this, as it serves the highest good of all. Sexual healing is real. So much damage has been enacted and passed along the lines of humanity. Some gentle, sweet, loving healing is in order.

▶ **Music.** Music was also not on my original list (another blind spot). Music is the voice of Spirit. Vibration is the language of the universe. I'm as far from a trained musician as perhaps anyone, but I now feel, know, and *innerstand* the magic of music. The goddess speaks from inside out. The drumbeat—pulse of our internal heartbeats—is a pathway home to the soul. However we can integrate music into our lives, the more powerful the healing we'll encounter. Music belongs to us all. However your voice sounds at first, however your timing feels—fuck it. Meet it with pure love. Do your dance. Sing your song. Bang your drum. You are eternally held.

► **Giving and service.** Life is all about service. When our well is full and our cup overflows, we are able to give and serve, which is what we are actually all about. Everything in nature serves the greater good. Apparently, even the humble human appendix (mine ruptured and I had it removed as a small child), which was believed to do "nothing" for the longest time, is in fact involved in repopulating gut microbes. Ha. When we give from a truly loving place, we activate our fundamental purpose—we incarnate to serve. Once we can accept our baseline safety on this earth, we have more than enough to give. Little warms the human heart as much as giving.

► **Receiving.** Again, not on my original list! The yin. And the balance to our giving. Being open to receiving is absolutely central to our wellness. And our disconnection with the goddess is the place where so many of us find ourselves disconnected for our ability to receive. Just like resting, sleeping, eating with peace, and enjoying sex, the yin is here waiting for us to remember the art of receptivity. Our human bodies process a lot. And in order to show up for service, we must be willing to receive in balance. How deep is your in-breath? What does it feel like to be truly nourished? The story that we've been told about having to prove our worth through productivity is leaving us spiritually, physically, and psychologically malnourished. Even those of us with plenty of money. The universe desires for us to receive with joy. We meet these gifts with gratitude, and the circle continues. Feeling worthy of receiving is the challenge and the opportunity for many of us. What does it feel like to receive the gift of beautiful music? To eat wonderful food? To receive a loving touch? Receiving is essential to our humanity and our way home.

- ▶ **Nature.** We are not separate from nature. What would it be like to commune with the Great Mother on a daily basis? To nurture a plant? To pet an animal? To breathe the air and remember that we are part of it? Everything on this list is part of nature. Everyone is part of nature. Drop all the way into the earth. We are inherently safe. The only thing in the way of us receiving all of her infinite gifts is us. All we need to do is slow down. Honor earth medicine. The answer to every question, ailment, and discomfort we have is to remember. Receiving the gifts of nature can feel like punishment when we are so programmed into forcing, prodding, and pushing away that we can't remember what universal love feels like. Universal love feels like bliss. And it's our birthright. Breathe into the Great Mother herself.

- ▶ **Spirit/Reflection.** Morning and evening rituals. Checking in at least once a day with our inner nature. Perhaps you're getting the point that all these things are the same thing. We are returning home. And home is eternal, benevolent, ever-loving bliss. Nothing stands in the way except for the programming and fear in our own minds. The source of so much of our pain is this disconnection. We replenish our wells by dropping in. At least once a day, remember. Just drop in, touch your heart, and choose love over fear. Every. Single. Day. Together, this love will turn the collective tide of fear into the possibility of love. Enchantment. Magic. The Mother.

LIVING A REGENERATIVE LIFE: PRACTICAL STEPS

Even the tiniest shifts, done daily, can change your entire life for the better. This can mean a one-minute-a-day singing practice. Committing myself to a regular meditation and writing practice has shifted my whole universe. Having a regular yoga practice has brought be more peace, health, and well-being than anything else I've ever done. Aligning with my life's purpose has brought me more joy than anything I've ever done. Finding happier, more mellow, more fulfilled spaces within ourselves also attracts like-hearted souls and helps us create a more balanced and connected outer world. Welcome to the future. Welcome to the now. Welcome to love.

Here are five simple inner work things that you can do right now to stand in your own ground, express your creativity, and start creating our future:

► **Start a spiritual practice.** It can be yoga once a week, five-minute meditations once a day, or even reading a spiritual book. Anything that connects you with the great blessed whatever. Practicing music and creating art count, as long as you are doing them in a state of connection, rather than judgment or perfectionism. Take up or return to something that brings you true joy, whether it be painting or pottery or dance. Honor the creative life force of the universe, no matter what it looks or sounds like. Let it rip. We want to see and hear what you've got!

► **Engage in inner inquiry.** It can be therapy rooted in Western psychology, coaching, an online course, or reading a book. Again, I highly recommend the work of Byron Katie. So much of what we do each day is unconscious. We need better tools to deal with our lives and deal with each other. Having better tools to deal with our emotions, our stressors, our grief, and our relationships makes life so, so much better.

▶ **Feel into your life's purpose, especially if you aren't 100 percent certain you are doing what you are here to do.** It's never too late or too early to find your path. Where you are is exactly perfect. Again, there are tons of resources online and in books—Julia Cameron's *The Artist's Way* is a wonderful starting point, and I also love Danielle LaPorte's *The Fire Starter Sessions* and *The Desire Map*. Joy comes from doing what you are here to do. Whatever that may be.

▶ **Slow down your breath. Breathe intentionally for at least one minute a day.** It's good for your nervous system. It's good for your spirit. Be in the moment. One helpful way to remember is to set alarms on your phone throughout the day. I know a startup CEO who would meditate for one minute per hour throughout the workday. Slow it down. Inhale. Pause. Exhale. Pause. Rinse. Repeat.

▶ **Move your body and spend time in nature.** Place your bare feet on the earth. Go hiking. Go surfing. Do yoga outside. Walk outside. Whatever feels good to you. There's no one correct way to do it. *Earthing: The Most Important Health Discovery Ever!* by Clinton Ober, Stephen Sinatra, and Martin Zucker is a useful primer on the benefits of putting bare feet on the earth. *The Earthing Movie: The Remarkable Science of Grounding* by Rebecca and Josh Tickell is also available for free on YouTube at the time of writing. To whatever extent possible, find your way toward natural light (sunlight, candles, fire) and limit exposure to electric light. Mind your soundscape, as well—the more natural sounds (crickets, birds) and the less car noise, the better. I also manage the scents in my life with an essential oil diffuser. *The Green Witch* by Arin Murphy-Hiscock is a beautiful primer on working with green energy.

Reconnecting to our roots, our inner worthiness, is no small task. At the same time, tiny steps toward inner integration can make a world of difference. Returning to the Mother is both the most challenging and the simplest thing we can possibly do. It requires tremendous courage to face inward and set down the armor we've all been taught to live with, and remembering our inherent power can take a little bit of practice. It runs directly up against just about everything the larger society has been forcing down our throats for all this time.

When in doubt, just breathe. Root. And remember.

SOUL SOIL EXERCISES

▶ Block out some time to go through the Living a Regenerative Life: Practical Steps list above and engage in a life assessment. How much of the goodness from this list are you receiving in life, and how much calls out to be integrated? Take out your journal and freewrite for at least ten minutes about what comes up.

▶ Focus on one of the above categories for a week. Where can you invite more yin, more

pleasure in your life? Reflect on how this
can help you create a regenerative life.

▶ Reflect on the idea and practice of living an
aligned, regenerative life. Where do you still feel
the pull of external validation, the urge to mine
or extract energy from yourself and the earth?
Reflect on the concept of energy in balance
and in flow, in harmony with nature. Freewrite
your feelings about this for at least ten minutes.

OUTER WORK

When it comes to outer work, changing our habits about what
we buy and eat, our actions in our neighborhoods and cities, and
our degree of support for organizations committed to human
rights and healing the soil are all direct ways to impact the world
at large. These steps may seem mundane in the face of the massive scale of climate change, but these are the brass tacks of life.

▶ **Support farmers that take care of the soil.** Vote with your
fork. Buy food from small farmers (directly or at farmers'
markets) and ask if they practice regenerative agriculture.
Talk to the farmers about their soil, and make sure they
are taking care of the microbial life and not using chemical
pesticides! You can also get their advice about your own
garden. Also, whenever possible, frequent restaurants that
support these farmers. Find out where the farmers sell their
food, and ask restaurants where they source their food.
Every single conversation on these matters contributes to
the larger movement. They signal to food producers that
people care what they are eating and are becoming more
educated about it. When you can't make it to the farmer's
market, buy organic. This does not guarantee that the

soil your food has been grown in is healthy, but it raises the odds quite a bit. It also guarantees that no industrial pesticides or herbicides have been used on your food and that you are not eating GMOs (genetically modified organisms). On that note, sell any stock you might have in companies that support or engage in destructive agriculture. If you can, buy stock in companies that are doing it right. As I've been writing this book, the world of regeneratively sourced products has grown. Patagonia has been a pioneer in the field, as well as Dr. Bronner's. Perfectly regenerative products are still a challenge at the time of writing, but more and more people are hard at work creating these businesses and products for the economy we all desire.

► **Give to organizations that replenish grasslands, agricultural land, and forests by healing the soil, as well as those that empower women and girls.** If your cup is overflowing, share the wealth. Donate to any organization working for healing grasslands through regenerative herding, protecting and healing forests and regenerating agricultural land, and those dedicated to helping women and girls around the world. Donate time and expertise to these organizations, including posting on social media, messaging and marketing, and contributing however you can to spread the word about the good work they do. As I've been writing this book, the world of regeneratively sourced products has grown. (Regeneration International, Kiss the Ground, and White Buffalo Land Trust are all wonderful options in this regard.)

► **Spread the word and encourage others to take these steps.** This matters! Educate yourself by looking at the resources I've provided. Then educate and enroll your friends, family, colleagues, and strangers in the movement. Are you a social media maven? Get on it! Do you have a blog or a speaking platform? Once you get yourself educated, start shouting it from the rooftops! And you don't need to be a soil scientist or an expert in anything. Just the simple message that the soil is alive and we need to protect it because it is connected to everything is incredibly powerful. Standing up for women and girls and supporting them is also vital to human survival, and the stories you share in this regard can be simple and direct. Own your voice and speak the truth. The most important thing to understand and communicate is that we have mission-critical solutions to climate change that don't require new or expensive technology, which is also a no-brainer for food and water security, for community, and for nature at large.

Remember that we are working with Mother Nature at every turn. Each small action makes a difference, and the intention with which we build our regenerative lives is building the new world. Co-create and vote for the world you desire to see with every action. Vote with your fork, but also with your money. Furthermore, vote with your vote! Grow food at home, be mindful whom you buy your food from, be mindful where you eat, support regenerative policies at all levels of government (making calls, spreading the word), vote in elections, and pass it on. Do yoga, meditate, or whatever else serves your inner self. Heal Spirit, earth, and body. Deepening your personal practice and education will fortify everything you say and do. Everything here is extremely doable, and every act in a positive direction makes a huge difference. This is how the tidal wave begins for the world we desire to create.

12

OWNING OUR POWER

Once we have strengthened and cleared our root chakra, we can step all the way into owning our power. Our ability to do our good in the world depends on our ability to hold our own center. Owning our power is about the inherent power within us. Again, most of us are taught our entire lives that our power is somehow outside of us. That we have to earn it and that it's defined by things that society dictates—looks, jobs, money, partners, and so on. Owning our power is about planting our feet on the ground, taking up space, and being heard. It's about knowing how much power we already hold within our own bodies and our own breath.

This phase of inner and outer works takes courage and commitment. Whenever I feel uncomfortable, I know I'm at my growth edge. Sweaty palms, the desire to crawl out of my skin and out of a situation, and physical shaking all characterize that *feeling like I'm going to die* feeling. It's the feeling most of us get before public speaking or performing, and in the world of personal and spiritual growth, it takes some getting used to. Most of us walk up to this edge and run the other way, back to our safety zone. But our edge is our frontier, and we are the pioneers, and in order to grow, we must venture out into the unknown, come what may.

I feel like I might pass out from this sort of discomfort at least once a day. I have enough creative and personal growth edges in my life (and people who actively invite me into my growth) that each day presents something new. It comes up when I'm about to work with a client I feel intimidated by, when I hit send or publish something I've written that's important to me, and with just about any form of creative exposure. It all inspires the fear of death in me. I realize that this sensation merely represents my ego's fear of death, and by now I am well practiced at working with my thought forms.

Recognizing that the ego mind is simply doing its job in response to my soul's growth and expansion helps tremendously. The bigger the expansion, the more convincing the fear response is. Recognizing also that even physical death is actually nothing to be afraid of in the grand scheme of the impermanence and life-death-rebirth cycles of nature also helps a great deal. Learning how to transmute this fear response into excitement and action is an art form in itself. Directly accepting and even loving the feeling of death is fertile soil for all creative work and self-expression. This expansion is what it takes to choose love over fear in a world where fear is still running the show. For decades, most of us have been living in a hyper-stimulated world without a lot of space for inner reflection, connection with nature, or slowing down.

One of the most jarring exercises I had to do in Bali during my yoga teacher training was to stand inside a circle of over twenty peers and announce, "I know my value. I honor my healthy boundaries." I stood there for several minutes weeping before I could even choke out the words. I realized that I had never actually practiced healthy boundaries and, furthermore, I had no sense of inherent worthiness that was not externally earned. I had been giving my power away in every way imaginable up until that point. And just about anyone could take it from me—in my studies, in my work, and in my relationships—because I hadn't the slightest idea that I was already an infinitely perfect expression of the universe exactly as I was.

I finally understood that if I thought I could earn my worthiness through work, money, looks, relationships, titles, or whatever, it meant that anyone without those things had to be less worthy than me. It created a trap where either I or the other person was *less than*. This is how we get into the comparison trap. All of capitalism relies on it. Patriarchy relies on it, too. The systems pillaging the planet rely on us not remembering who we truly are, because if we were all to wake up simultaneously, the castle built on sand would immediately crumble and fall.

The fragmentation of the goddess has also left us rudderless, denied the complete picture and lied to about the whole story. Our power lies in our remembering and reclaiming what was taken from us. Thankfully, the truth is already within us. When we take our cues from nature and remember that we are pieces of the inherent perfection of nature, we can remember our true power. The fact that the root chakra is the perfect metaphor for everything that ails us collectively is not a coincidence. The universe is perfect, alive, loving, and co-creative, and also has a sense of humor.

BOUNDARIES AND COMMUNICATION

We can't talk about the root chakra and owning our power without talking about boundaries. Boundaries and communication are the bridge between us owning our power and us moving within the world. It's all about speaking our authentic truth and standing in our integrity.

Our boundaries are formed by saying *yes* and *no*. By our ability to speak our needs and have them honored. They can be flexible, like personal space, and are not the same thing as having and holding walls between ourselves and others. Healthy boundaries require a connection with the throat chakra and speaking our truth about our bodies, our time, our space, our needs, and our desires.

Originally designed for peacemaking in the 1960s, I've found Marshall Rosenberg's NVC (Nonviolent Communication) to be an incredibly powerful approach. This method offers individuals tools for neutrally communicating their needs, feelings, and desires without emotional manipulation and codependency. It also focuses on taking responsibility for emotions, actions, and choices, while communicating with honesty, empathy, and compassion. Nonviolent Communication is a significant antidote to the blaming, shaming, controlling, and comparing language that fuels destructive forms of patriarchal organization. Boundaries and communication are where the rubber meets the road of owning our truth, speaking it, and communicating our needs.

We keep our hearts open while honoring our healthy boundaries by owning our power. When we own our power, nobody and nothing can be a threat to us. Our sacred yes and our sacred no come naturally and intuitively. Nothing needs to be forced, because there is no fear. It can take some adjustment when the standing culture is massively codependent and the tendencies of that culture are mistaken for being normal. Again, these are the workings of patriarchy, and they require us to untangle and deprogram ourselves from within. Owning our power with healthy boundaries and clear communication creates the solid structure for our feminine, sacral energy to express and play.

PLAY, LIGHTNESS, LAUGHTER, CREATIVITY, AND THE UNEXPECTED

Here, we enter a space where owning our power, communicating well, holding heartfelt boundaries, and incorporating play and creativity all converge. Sacred sexuality and the sacral chakra also teach us that the universe is creative and wants us to play. Laugher and silliness are some of the most effective healing balms around.

Through my throat, sacral, and root chakra openings, I've found so many places where the universe is begging me to play. A couple of years ago, I picked up the guitar that I'd been schlepping around for years and finally started to learn a few chords. Now little brings me as much joy as messing around with it and not worrying about what it sounds like. I also allow myself to be ridiculous in attempting freestyle rap as a vocal exercise, and the resulting silliness has led to hours of crying laughter (it's also done wonders for my personal expression in writing, business, and public speaking).

My sexual exploration, guitar, and freestyle rap sessions may seem like a far cry from what it will take to address the climate emergency, but there's no way for us to integrate our relationship with the earth unless we directly relate with our own energies, voices, and bodies. The great news is that while we have serious work to do, the universe itself wants us to be embodied, alive, joyous, and connected while we are doing it. Even in the act of writing this book, the universe no longer allows me to create from a mindest of struggle. Every word is a celebration. And everything that pours into this expression is a universal party that exudes the love, joy, creativity, and abundance of the universe.

SACRED SEXUALITY: THE CREATIVE LIFE FORCE OF THE UNIVERSE

From the basics of our power, our boundaries, and our communication, we rise into the next level of creative expression. Just as with the root chakra, connecting to our sacral chakra is necessary if we want to heal our relationship with the soil and the planet. The severing of us humans from our lower chakras has left us unrooted, disembodied, and without our natural connection to the sacred sexual. We have, instead, been taught that Spirit is all about some ephemeral notion in the sky, and that our earthly bodies and souls are marked by original sin: the outrageous notion that we are inherently flawed and broken from the day we are born. We have been taught to feel guilt and shame about our sexuality, but it is actually our most beautiful gift and one of our most primary connections with the divine.

Healing the sacral chakra means reconnecting to our healthy sexual energy, sensuality, and creativity. The sacrum, located at the base of the spine, is derived from the Latin for "sacred bone," as it was believed the soul resided here. Kundalini ("coiled snake" in Sanskrit) is believed to be a feminine, sexual, serpent-like energy that is coiled at the base of the spine until it is awakened, wherein it rises through the chakras in the central column of the body. The snake has been a symbol of the divine feminine, Great Mother, and Shakti energy all over the world since ancient times. Vilified (along with Lilith) in the story of Adam and Eve, it remains a universal symbol for transformation, death, and rebirth (the shedding of the skin).

Our sexuality is our direct line to the divine. It follows our energetic roadmap and is the source of our creative play, desire, and pleasure. Saying yes to our sexuality and learning how to harness the beauty within allows the universe to flow through us and express. Unlocking, releasing, and untangling the conditioned suppression around our sexuality is an essential key to unleashing our personal freedom, joy, fulfillment, and creative expression.

The creative life force of the universe is playful. The soul wants to play; the ego wants to play small. Our creativity is our birthright, and our desires point us to where our highest selves want to go. My own personal healing journey with sexuality has provided me with some of the most opening conversations, honest interactions, and vulnerable connections of my life. When we can shed the guilt, suppression, and shame of two thousand years of patriarchal conditioning that we have inherited around our sexuality since sexual healers were separated from their roles as priestesses and turned into celibate nuns, we can begin to return to the power, wonder, and play of our whole sexual selves.

Look closely at an image of the Virgin of Guadalupe. You might notice a beautiful yonic symbol (a vagina) staring back at you. The. Great. Mother. The "vagin" Mary. Hidden in plain sight. Just like the soil. Speaking of Marys, *The Magdalen Manuscript* brings forward the story of Mary Magdalen as Jesus's lover and spiritual partner—a sexual healing priestess from the line of Isis.[1] Written into the patriarchal history as a prostitute, we've inherited Christianity's caricature of women as either celibates or prostitutes. The Madonna/whore syndrome. This line to our sexuality was broken and brutally suppressed because it is our *life force*, our *birthright*.

The creative life force of the universe is reproductive, fertile, sensual, playful, and sexy. Our disconnection from the incredible source of our infinite universal worthiness and power is keeping us from remembering who we are and what is possible. This life force is also directly connected to our voices, as our root and sacral chakras are connected through creative energy to our throat chakras. Song, vibration, music, and manifestation come from this connection. As we connect our lower chakras to the upper, we are able to dance with the rainbow and tap into universal intelligence. We are powerful beyond our wildest imagination. We are infinite.

As we remember the Mother Goddess, we remember her role in fertility. I'm always blown away by the number of seeds that plants produce. Each basil plant, for example, produces hundreds when it goes to seed. It only needs one to replace itself, yet it produces more than enough for a person to save for years and years' worth of basil plants. Magical. And the seeds that don't become new plants or get collected for the future return to the earth and go back into the cycle: nothing wasted. What is meant to germinate and grow will grow, and all else will be returned to the cycle. Profound abundance. I'm pretty sure the goddess is hiding in your compost heap. The secret is in the perfect design of things as they work together.

Each personal expression of the sacred sexual is different. That's part of the abundant diversity of nature. There's no one-size-fits-all answer to what will serve the highest good of any individual. But there's transformative power in self-love and giving ourselves permission, as well as rescinding authority from any entity that wants to lay claim to our bodies, our pleasure, our expression, and our reproductive rights. Our joy, our pleasure, and our bodies belong to us.

BRINGING IT ALL TOGETHER: WITCHES, PLANT MEDICINE, AND SEX

Somehow, the most beautiful, prolific, and magical aspects of life have become the most vilified. We are terrified of plant medicine, magical women, and unbridled sexuality. What is this wild disjuncture about? Why would the most joyous and free aspects of human life be the most controlled? Why have motherhood, sexuality, fertility, and dance such a long history of being suppressed? What in the world is going on when the simplest joys humanity can experience are the sources of the most pain, fear, and suppression?

Speaking about witches as wise women, plant medicine as nature speaking truth, and sex as the grand expression of life has inspired far more fear than I could have imagined. My journey has triggered just about everybody who has crossed my path. But the goddess is always here, dancing and gyrating, loving, and whispering sweet poetry, as I also feel something unconscious and unnatural programmed inside me clench down and try to control the nectar flowing through me.

Witches, of course, have always been healers, herbalists, and wise, wild women. One of the legends in this field is Clarissa Pinkola Estés and her archetypal history in *Women*

Who Run With the Wolves: Myths and Stories of the Wild Woman Archetype. Estés writes of freedom and the ways it's been suppressed, as well as modes of inner knowing through ancestral stories and powerful archetypes. The patriarchal reaction to divine feminine wildness has been violent and insidious. The horror of witch hunts was real—gruesome physical and psychological torture, as well as unimaginable forms of murder. The witch wound is very alive today. Those hunts were the physical manifestation of the metaphorical destruction of the dark goddess, the moon goddesses, and the earth and fire goddesses. The crone archetype (of the ancient and worldwide maiden, mother, and crone triad) was co-opted by patriarchy and profoundly demonized (becoming the father, the son, and the who-what-now?). The wheel of the year, honoring the cycles of nature and the movement of the moon and sun, was also co-opted and deformed into mainstream religious holidays (e.g., Easter and Halloween). Even the word *pagan* carries derogatory undertones that were created specifically to undermine earth-based spirituality.

This isn't ancient history. The present-day persecution of women and girls continues in force worldwide. Assaults on reproductive rights and misogynist rape culture continue. Disgustingly, women were systematically turned against each other during the witch hunts, and we see the legacy of this today in rampant mean girl culture. Women shame and exclude each other unconsciously to maintain their position in a patriarchal system, all while railing against patriarchy. Don't be fooled—that's by design. The system requires that we remain unconscious and separated so that we keep perpetuating it. The way out is to wake up and remember.

Standing in the identity of *witch* is dangerous and triggering to this day. In *Waking the Witch: Reflections on Women, Magic, and Power*, Pam Grossman guides us through the evolution of the witch archetype over time. Her answer is that the witch is at once a symbol of feminine power and female oppression.[2] While the word has been used as a slur in an attempt to defile women, it continues to be reclaimed and reimagined, and a woman's power lies in the interplay. A witch can reclaim her magic by reclaiming her title. That's her trick. That's her treat. It's utterly maddening to the mind that needs to control what is. She slips past. She shimmies through. She will not be tamed. She will not be contained. And the rage and fear that she inspires is ultimately not up to her. She's not worried about your trigger. She doesn't care if you find her light, her power, her voice, her creativity, her sexuality, her knowing, her wisdom, her freedom, her expression, her body, or her magic threatening. She simply rises.

MAGIC

While we're talking about witches, let's talk about magic. Knowledge of herbs and plants has always been an essential part of human spirituality and our relationship with the earth. The practice of employing food as medicine is ancient, as is the use of plants for spiritual ceremony and healing.

Additionally, ancient knowledge regarding the menstrual cycle has helped us connect to our bodies and work with our hormones, body knowing, and sensitivity for thousands and thousands of years. The amount of culturally transmitted shame regarding menstruation reflects the patriarchy's enduring disdain and fear of the magic within. People who don't physically bleed can also sync up with the moon and move with the cycles of nature. We all have so much magic available to us within our bodies and within nature, but the only way to access it is to connect with it. We actually deny our own magic by denying ourselves. Ritual, non-Western healing modalities, the use of mantras, and indigenous forms of music are all making a comeback, but not without being ridiculed and sidelined as woo by the patriarchy (including the patriarchy enacted by women).

Forms of understanding the cosmos, our relationship to the sky, and our relationship to Spirit are also making a comeback. Astrology offers us an archetypal map of our lives and everyone else's, and tarot provides a language through which Spirit can communicate (or through which we can communicate with our highest selves, which is also Spirit). Divination, of course, makes no sense if we believe the universe is inert and we are simply made of matter, untethered from Spirit. It requires a relationship to a living, co-creative universe, and an understanding of ourselves as Spirit, as well as everything else, for the connection and the magic to make sense and actually work.

The plant-based, healing, spiritual wisdom of indigenous cultures has also been co-opted and attacked to this day, including through torture and genocide. If we think about what the expression of patriarchy through the fear-based ego was trying to accomplish to begin with (i.e., to subdue humans), all the killing and torture to reinforce a disconnect with our own power, magic, and the universe makes sense. Given that sexuality is the creative life force of the universe and our direct connection to Spirit, it's not at all surprising that the violent oppression of non-male sexuality goes hand in hand with the destruction of our soils, land, indigenous peoples, women and girls, and the rest of the natural world. Our disconnection with the Great Mother, creatrix of all things, is at the spiritual, moral, philosophical, political, and practical heart of the mess we're in.

In *Sacred Geometry: Philosophy and Practice*, Robert Lawlor outlines the relationship between the vibrational reality of all things and the ancient evolution of mathematics via geometry. He posits that our original relationship with geometry is feminine. What if there were an ancient resonance within all things, inescapable and undeniable? What if the fabric of all of life could be felt in music, dance, sexuality, sensuality, art, and nature? Terence McKenna famously directs us back to the Eleusinian Mysteries and the cults of mushroom worship around the world in *Food of the Gods: The Search for the Original Tree of Knowledge—A Radical History of Plants, Drugs, and Human Evolution*. McKenna posits that human consciousness itself is directly tied to our prehistoric relationship with mushrooms. The Vestal Virgins (mentioned earlier) were priestesses, healers, and ceremonial guides. Pre-patriarchy—before our divide from the Great Mother (feminine Shakti wisdom)—was intrinsic to society's relationship with itself. Fertility, food, abundance, sexuality, creativity, childbirth, child rearing, death, beauty, and expression—all of these were the realm of the great creatrix. Layne Redmond describes extensive priestess cultures in which women acted as shamans, guides, and healers in order to connect society with the divine in *When the Drummers Were Women: A Spiritual History of Rhythm*. She details how priestesses and their sacred drums were banned when earth-based spirituality gave way to monotheistic organized religion a few thousand years later, and outlines how sexual healing distorted into celibacy for those would become nuns and priests.

Plant medicine, ceremony, healing sound, herbalism, and female healing modalities became banned, dismantled, and suppressed by force. Eventually, the once-sacred knowledge and honor of the female menstruation cycle became shamed, denied, and hidden, and reproductive health and childbirth were handed over to an overwhelmingly male dominated medical system. The coining of the term *witch*, the European witch hunts, and the concept of the devil were all born in the clash between the burgeoning church, its political and economic motivations, and the violent shift from earth-based spirituality to monotheistic patriarchal religion and society. Our connection to the earth, Spirit, each other, and our bodies, as well as to the subconscious and dream states, broke down under the weight of it all. Colonialism was both a source and a result of this breakdown. To this day, indigenous people are brutally suppressed, threatened, and harmed all over the world, being taken by force and mined for resources.

It should come as no surprise that the US is built on a Western myth in which Zeus rapes Hera by using her own empathy against her. Think about how our food system depends upon synthetic chemical inputs rather than natural compost, and how it depends on low-wage labor by people of color in terrible working conditions, and how we rely on fossil fuels and truckers working overtime to ship everything we could ever want from around the world. The reality of this profound and grotesque injustice must be exposed. And the millennia of physical, psychological, and spiritual violence must be exposed with it, along with the rage and grief that are just beginning to see the light of day.

We've all had to internalize parts of the patriarchal narrative to survive and stay alive. It's no longer specifically about gender or even race, and even these very constructs are controlled functions of patriarchy. Our entire systems of knowing—including academia and the arts—are permeated by patriarchy. Our whole economy is defined by patriarchy.

The beginnings of the end of patriarchy are only the starting place for what promises to be a new world. If we can transcend the incredible and unthinkably urgent challenge of the climate catastrophe and physically survive to see the new new age, that is. The good news is that because the broken part of this system is our connection to Spirit, healing our connection to Spirit (within ourselves) is where the greatest (and, in my opinion, only) hope lies. Healing our connection to the soil as fertile feminine is the same thing as healing our connection to ourselves, each other, our home, our magic, our innate power, our hope, the present, the past, and the future.

What if the truth were staring us right in the face? What if the truth were always underfoot? In our cells and in our bones? Thankfully, nonlinear time allows us to turn and heal on a dime.

We have everything we need to return home and reclaim our birthright of worthiness. None of this relies on academic arguments about anything. Instead, it all relies on the breath, the pulse, the drumbeat, and our deepest inner knowing. Our remembering is embodied. The truth is unfuckwithable. The Great Mother's song is infinite and rising.

13

WHAT'S POSSIBLE

What's possible is us waking up to the truth of interconnection. What's possible is reconnecting to where our food comes from— worldwide—as well as the healing of our agricultural system. Doing this will ripple out, heal the economy, and help us with the twin problems of obesity and malnutrition. What's possible is clean drinking water, more biodiversity, and healing our oceans. This will take a good deal of relatively simple action. It doesn't live in the technological future, and it's not at all more than we can afford within our existing economic structure. It's well within our reach and it would be absolute folly to do anything other than to take focused, concerted action starting right now in every way possible to move this train forward. Yes? Yes.

SOUL MEETS SUSTAINABILITY

Let's walk forward together feeling alive, satisfied, enriched, and inspired. Remember, institutions do not lead; they follow. Institutions are just groups of people with sets of agreements. When those agreements fall apart, the institutions fall apart. When we make new agreements, new institutions are formed. Now, people and institutions do tend to be path-dependent, meaning they tend to keep doing whatever they are already doing until something disrupts the path. We are told that institutions are difficult to move and change, and in many ways they are, but we forget that they simply follow the lead of what is demanded of them. Corporations, for example, can only sell what people buy. If we change our minds about what we're going to buy, corporations will unequivocally change what they sell. It has already happened untold times throughout the course of modern history. The organic food industry, for example, crossed the $50 billion mark in 2018 and continues to grow along with awareness.[1] The emperor has no clothes, my friends.

We have no good reason to not work to heal our soil. And we do this by doing it. It's that simple. We bring the future that we want into being by setting a clear intention and then doing it. If you have practiced setting intentions in your own life, you were probably blown away by what you were able to create by simply getting clear on what you wanted to do and then moving forward to execute that intention. The same process works at every level—individual, city, state, national, and international. The Universal Declaration on Human Rights, although still a work in progress, put a stake in the ground for a collective intention and changed world forever by laying a foundation of agreed upon values after two catastrophic world wars. The Declaration is still cited and invoked around the world, and it plays an important role in international law. So far, our collective progress has been slowed considerably by the patriarchal influence baked into our institutions, but we can get a glimmer of what's possible. During World War II, more than 40 percent of all produce came from individual *victory gardens*, grown by people on their own land, although this too has a dark history of stolen land and Japanese and German internment. We can do better by seeing what's possible and actively disassembling patriarchy through *decolonization gardens*, *climate victory gardens*, or *new world gardens*, or whatever we desire.

Growing our own food is healthier, more financially sustainable, more joyful, and way more carbon friendly than purchasing food from other sources. Even growing a few tomato plants and some herbs can brighten our days and give us something nutritious (and nearly free). Also, in the abundant nature of the Mother, each tomato yields seeds we can collect and grow even more plants with, and, as I covered earlier, a number of plants can be regrown in just half an inch of water by keeping their ends. My little indoor basil plant and my outdoor rosemary bush regularly add flavor to my meals. I've also found that simple, hardy plants lend a sense of security and well-being from their steady, nourishing presence. And as if that weren't enough, there are all sorts of indoor plants that will help clean the air in our spaces. Any beginner can start small and learn just about everything to get going on YouTube.

While I know this truth is worthy of catching fire, right now it's at a slow burn. The issues of soil and agriculture made a strong showing at COP21 in Paris, the path-breaking international climate change meeting in early December 2015. The French government's proposal for all countries to increase their soil carbon by 0.4 percent (which would translate to billions of tons of carbon drawn down from the atmosphere if applied worldwide) took hold and was signed by dozens of countries and organizations. While it flew under the mainstream radar, this agreement marked a major step in the journey to creating actionable steps for governments, farmers, organizations, and individuals around the world.

THE POWER OF COLLECTIVE INTENTION

One of the biggest takeaways from my dissertation about whether or not urban sustainability plans affect outcomes is that yes, they do. Plans are essentially collective intentions. They stake a claim, and then to be in integrity, city officials must put their money where their intention is. And in each case that I studied, they did. It's a bit like saying out loud to friends and family when your book draft will be done. The internal intention, backed up by public accountability, opens up the path for the goal to be completed. And when goals are not being met, it shines a light on what might be missing.

The other day, a friend of mine sent me one of those inspirational viral memes with a quote by Greg Reid:

> A dream written down with a date becomes a goal.
> A goal broken down into steps becomes a plan.
> A plan backed by action makes your dreams come true.

So, for any cynics in the audience who may be sold on the basic premise of healing the soil to balance out the carbon cycle but aren't yet ready to believe it can actually be done, this is the way forward. In order to create anything, somebody must first believe in it and be willing to fight for it. Not only fight for it, but also initiate and see it through to completion. This is as true in the entrepreneurial world as it is in the policy and artistic worlds.

This work of healing the soil is thoroughly divine. And so is every piece of art, and every piece of research that moves science forward, and every act of advocacy, and so on. All work that involves creating something is creative work. And all creation is divine.

> The great lessons from the true mystics, from the Zen monks . . . is that the sacred is in the ordinary, that it is to be found in one's daily life, in one's neighbors, friends, and family, in one's back yard, and that travel may be a flight from confronting the sacred . . . To be looking elsewhere for miracles is to me a sure sign of ignorance that everything is miraculous.[2]
> ABRAHAM MASLOW

Let's imagine a world in which we have more nutritious food, more food for the world, more clean water, less runoff, healthier ecosystems, and less carbon in our atmospheres and oceans. Healthy soil creates all these things. Rather than zeroing in on climate change, let's instead envision ourselves righting the whole system. It's possible to create what we want on this planet. To put it back into balance, we only have to understand the basics and then take action.

Let's imagine a world where we compost instead of using pesticides and fertilizers. Let's create a world where we understand the importance of fungi and work with them instead of against them. Where women and girls are truly supported and protected. Let's create a vision that is in line with love and connectedness and good food. And then let's execute on that vision. Let's create regenerative lives and a regenerative world. We live in a realm of infinite possibility. We've been doing it wrong for a while now, but that's okay—we can correct our course. It won't happen by accident, though. We actually have to focus on what needs to change and then take the steps to change it. We take care of soil, we take care of ourselves, we take care of each other. We're all one.

This is a clear call to action. There are things every one of us can do today to start to right the system. If we normally go to the supermarket and buy whatever without giving it a second thought, we can instead choose to pay attention to where our food comes from. At the very least we can buy organic, and support farmers' markets, too. If we have the opportunity to ask our farmers about their soil, we do. And ultimately we grow our own food, knowing firsthand where it comes from and saving transport costs and gas.

Growing our own food is an act of revolution. We must get back to our roots. Back to the basics. We must realize limitation in order to transcend it. Dig in. Dig deep. Do the work. And receive. Acknowledge what we're pretending not to know. Our work will require changing our systems from the inside, and it will require changing our lives and ourselves from the inside. Changing our behaviors regarding what we buy and eat, how we participate in our neighborhoods and cities, and how we support organizations and policy change devoted to healing the soil and empowering women in the United States will actually change the world.

I was talking to my dad one day about American politics, and he passionately pointed out that the people who talk about "making it on their own" seem to have no concept of how much they actually rely on the government—roads and bridges, the military, child labor laws, and the forty-hour work week, just to name a few examples. I took it a step further and reminded him that the government didn't just arbitrarily decide to start working on these things of its own accord; people fought for each of these issues, giving their lives for the cause in a number of instances. They were people like you and me who looked around and decided that the status quo was not good enough. People who decided to do something about it, and to reshape government in such a way that it reflected their values.

Published in 1962, the book *Silent Spring* left a lasting mark on America and the world. In it, Rachel Carson details the dangers of pesticides in poisoning lawns and fields and the bodies of animals and humans. The notion of a silent spring referred to a spring with no robins, as the eggs of robins were emerging too thin to sustain the lives of baby birds, and thus a generation of songbirds were exchanged for a blanket of pesticides in the US. The book invoked the ire of the chemical and pesticide industries, and they relentlessly attacked Carson for being hysterical and ignorant of science. But despite their protests, a chord was struck with the American public—especially with American mothers.

American mothers are, as a cohort, by far the largest food purchasers in the country and in the world. They choose what America eats, they run homeowners' associations, and they vote.

If every mother in America decided to make a small set of different choices at the dinner table and diverted some food purchasing to small garden growing, the whole world would change very quickly. And, as happened after *Silent Spring* was published, if these mothers turn their passion to politics, path-breaking laws will be enacted and shit will get done. *Silent Spring* is largely credited as a major instigator in the public awareness and outcry around environmental pollution in the sixties, leading to the National Environmental Policy Act, as well as other far-reaching environmental protections.

The Great Mother is pouring through our collective psyche. None of this is an accident or a coincidence. We are facing our own extinction, our own demise, because we have been blind to humanity's deepest truths within us. We desire better than this. We know how to get there. It's in our bones. It's both simple and complex. We are remembering. It requires courage to face the truth—the truth within ourselves, within our own hearts. The light and love that illuminate our inevitable pathway home. Breathe. Find your feet. Find your heartbeat. Drop in to the eternal love guiding us all.

SOUL SOIL EXERCISES

► Set some intentions for yourself at the next new moon. Make a list of whatever feels comfortable that you can commit to. This doesn't have to be in goal form—you can intend to breathe more deeply each day or commit to a specific practice. Check in with your intentions at the following full moon. Take out your journal and freewrite for at least ten minutes about what comes up. You can also set intentions for longer timeframes as you get comfortable.

► Reflect on aligning your food purchasing, food growing, and political activism. Where could you show up in small ways? Where could you show up in bigger ways? Freewrite your feelings about this for at least ten minutes.

14

THE DIVINE DANCE

The dance of the divine feminine and masculine. It's what everything's about at the end of the day. What if we could tap into the divine balance of all things? What would a society that didn't involve arguing even look like?

I have spent so much of my time on earth worried about being right. And as my cells turn over and the divine dance of all things continues and I remember my humble mortality, I remember the truth of love. Running through all things. Inhabiting every creature. The energetic life force of the universe. The truth, as it seems, cannot be contained. The universe speaks. The Great Mother herself speaks in every breath.

A few years back (after a major faceplant), I sat with my friend Dream (yes, that's her real name) and cried, "I just want to be a normal person." She cackled, "How's that working out for ya, Erin?" I had just been through a brutal breakup and had my book rejected by the publisher I thought was the one. The truth was, I wasn't showing up all the way. In my playing it safe, I was getting my ass handed to me. The second I turned that spiritual corner, I found my agent and paved the way to the eventual publication of the book you're holding now. I quadrupled down on the dark goddess and gave my spiritual ooph my all. All the divine needed was my *fuck yes*. I had to put my back into it. *Maybe* was not going to cut it any more. I had to step all the way into my authentic truth, into my power. There was no other way. In the same way, the Great Mother is ready for our *fuck yes*.

For all the difficulty of this moment facing the climate emergency, life is about celebration. Celebrating our authentic voices, sharing our gifts, dancing with the give and take in the balance of all things. The Mother needs our *fuck yes*. There is no other way. While the state of the earth is dire, the healing balm we need is actually the path of love and interconnectedness. Calling in and weaving back together the lost parts of ourselves is the way forward. There is no halfway here. There is no looking away.

LISTENING TO DIVINE INTELLIGENCE

When we connect our third eye and crown chakras, we connect with our clear seeing and are able to receive from divine intelligence. Magic derives from this ability to tune in to the intelligence that is way greater, faster, and smarter than our little egos and brains ever could be. With healthy boundaries, we are also able to tap into the collective consciousness without getting lost in it. We all have superpowers latent within our bodies that connect us from above and below. Drawing light and power down into the earth and drawing energy up from the earth allows us to expand and create with ease and brilliance that can only be attributed to the divine.

In this way, we are divine vessels. We show up and our souls incarnate with a perfect map and ongoing guidance and instructions. The word *surrender* in this context means to drop in and surrender to universal directions. This entire book is an exercise in such following of directions. They often make no sense from a purely material perspective, and the surrender element comes in trusting the benevolent universe in the perfection of its creative intelligence. The fibonacci sequence on the bottom of a pinecone or the center of a sunflower is a perfect example of this divine coding and expression. Nature is perfect. All the information we need is in our DNA. The Mother is all-knowing. The universe is communicating with us all the time; we just need to be listening.

As it relates to the climate and other major challenges we face on earth right now, following this divine intelligence is the only way to actually navigate these waters. Our egocentric, disconnected, hyper-mental approach is exactly how we got into this situation to begin with. We must remember that nature is perfectly efficient and brilliant, and way smarter than us. We need only to work with nature and follow her directions, remembering that we are part of her—always have been and always will be. Drop in to the flow.

The process of losing our connection with the Great Mother, society by society, fundamentally broke the connection between women, the womb, childbirth, child rearing, menstruation, healthy sexuality, autonomy, the elements, home, the land, the harvest, the moon, fertile soil, and food. Sacred sexuality, sound healing and vibration, breathwork, and plant medicine have always been at the center of embodied spirituality. Spirituality is actually about our relationship with our own bodies, our own energy, our own sexuality, the earth upon which we walk, the stars above, and the love we have for each other. It's about our internal truth, personal power, creative joy, inherent wholeness, balance of feminine and masculine energies, and connection with all that is.

The ego's desire to control is universal. It shapes the lenses we look through as we create our lives. At the end of the day, the only thing true is love. I understand how upsetting the obviousness of these truths are, especially when we've been denying ourselves over and over again. Especially when we feel like we are in service to the earth, but something always seems to be missing. Coming out of the spiritual closet is an actual thing.

The infinite wisdom of the universe is so far beyond all of our silly little human selves. All we can do is kneel. Pray. Be humble and do our best to learn and listen. Remember all the incredible power that lies within each of us. We incarnated to do this. We belong here. We are children of the earth and we have a role to play in the Great Awakening. Everything is perfect. As Lindsay Mack often says, we cannot miss what is meant for us.

RISE AND REMEMBER

Together, we rise. Together, we remember. Together, we take back what is ours, call our power back collectively, and retrieve our souls from all the places we've abandoned ourselves. The ancestors, angels, and guardians are all on team love. As we awaken and begin to act in love and harmony, more and more souls will remember. And as we remember, we collectively root down and bring balance back to the cycles of nature.

This was never complicated. The solutions to what seem like intractable problems are already within us. While we get to show up in integrity and action, we do not need to suffer in constructing the world and the new institutions that our souls are calling for. We all know the way. In every cell in our bodies. In every dream, every relationship, every piece of art, dance, and song. We know. We have always known. Welcome back to the Mother. To the truth. To the only thing there ever was. Welcome back to wholeness. Feel the sacred vibration from root to crown. The answers, the actions. The love is already here. We are made of love and there is no other truth.

Listen to the drumbeat, the heartbeat, that calls us all. Move toward the light, and know that this earth is stacked with guides—souls prepared, willing, and ecstatic to be here in service to humanity's great awakening. If you ever feel lost, find the earth. Find your breath. Call out for support. To the great divine, to the Mother, to the ether. Find your feet. Release what does not serve. Find the earth fully supporting your body and know that you are eternally safe. Breathe. We were born ready. We arrived for this. Welcome home.

Use your voice. Your sacred vibration. Your manifesting power. Find your feet and speak your truth in your highest integrity. When you need to rest, rest. When you get up, get back to work. Gently, humbly, regeneratively, in highest service to all that is. What do we do? We do whatever we can. We do whatever it takes. We support and love each other. We follow sound and light and call out to guides when lost. But we are never truly lost. We are always exactly where we need to be. Where do we start? We start where we are. We must be where we are before we can be anyplace else.[1] Don't despair. Everything we need is here. We follow the breath. We travel light, and everything we need will be provided exactly as we need it.

Remember who you are and why you incarnated. You belong. You are worthy. You are infinitely powerful. Use this power for the highest good of all. We've got this. Breathe. Step. Remember. Believe. Join hands. Transcend. Find your vision and stubbornly walk, step after step, toward it. Ignore naysayers. Offer your grace. Be who you were born to be. There is no higher calling. You are it. We are it. Let's do this.

One hand on your heart, one hand on your root, take three cleansing breaths. Offer gratitude for wherever you are in this moment and whatever has been provided for you. Drop in to the moment. Drop in to your root. Remember. Share. Show up in service. Keep your intention toward the light and you can never go wrong. Bless. None of us are saints. We are humans humaning. Some shit gets messy. All we can do is face inward, be true to ourselves and others, honor our healthy boundaries, and know our value. Return, return, return. Remember, remember, remember. Love, love, love.

Let there be peace. Imagine what's possible. Every single day. Tune in to infinite possibility. Join hands. Collaborate. Share stories. Share food and drink. Create. Laugh. Love. Pray, however that works for you. Together we have more than enough power to change these tides. Listen closely. And follow directions even when they seem crazy. Society has been crazy, not us. We breathe. We walk, we step, we create, we believe. We don't need to fight. We breathe and step. We insist. We generate. The world we know is possible.

May we all move forward with the following blessing:

May we understand our own deep interconnectedness to all things. May our actions align with the highest good of our inner selves and of all things in the universe. May we bless all money that moves in and out of our lives so that it may serve the highest good of all. May we bless all food that moves in and out of our bodies so that it may serve the highest good of all. May we remember our true nature and remember that we are part of nature. May our disagreements serve only to increase understanding, knowledge, and well-being. May love replace fear everywhere and lead to all institutions rising to the highest good of all. May truth, peace, and love prevail. And so it is.

ACKNOWLEDGMENTS

To the Great Mother, the plant, animal, and fungi kingdoms. To the sacred song and the ancient vibrations that are life itself. To the great goddesses and Team Highest Good, my spirit team.

My deepest gratitude to my family, who have seen me through every stage of this remarkable journey. To my parents, Julian, Elise, Audrey, Mae, Dee-Dee, extended family, grandparents, ancestors, and loved ones on the other side. In particular, Lo-Lo and Lo-Ya, Josephine, Grandad, Big Granny, and Pa. To Luna cat, the biggest badass around.

To my book doula and soul sister, Monica, I don't know who I would be without you. To my agent, Amanda, for believing in me and what's possible for our world. To my editors, Diana and Robert, and the Sounds True team for saying yes to this book and helping me shape it into what it is today.

To all those who supported this book in its earliest stages. A special thanks to Paul and Cheryl J. Marshall for your incredible support. To my PhD committee, David, Tridib, and Manuel. To Lauren, Jonas, Ryland, Finian, and the original Kiss the Ground team for bringing all of this to life. To Stacie and Andrew for being stewards of the sacred land we live on and holding space for my growth. To Alyssa for incredible support and being in highest service. To Zoë, Tish, Jake, and Andrew for being the magical family you are. To all of LP 122, buddy Felix, and the feelies. Jayden Lee, Caroline, Chad, Sab, Sanjay, Mariana, and Mark. To TLA, especially Thomas and Matthew, for support.

To Allison K., for the cry of all women. To Cat Kabira and my yoga lovelies. To the Kern Family Farm. To Jimmy, Jackie, and the Duke's Ohana. To the Beautiful Writer's Group.

To dear friends and loved ones who have been here the whole way. To Zach P. for walking with me, seeing me, and remembering spirit partnership. To Joy A., Sara, Andrew, Gemma, Ashton, Naccole, Brad P., Ben F., Mark N., Delaney, Eli, and Agnes for friendship. To Tom for unwavering support. To Nirvan for creative inspiration. To Dream for dreaming. To Ian R., Sarah P., Zach M., Angie, June, Winn, Kristen A., Stephen and Gaya, Joy R., Gigi, Angela, Henry, Eduardo, Dougie, Ashley, and Basecamp for your magic, vision, and collaboration. To Jane M. for your magical guidance.

To my crowdfunding supporters—you made this possible: Thomas Brodahl, Steven Starr, Sara Walshe, Robert Bailey, Justin Brown, Don Smith, Jessica L. Johnson, Carmelo Gandia, Alexa Giuffre, Petra Ostermuenchner, Jayden Lee, Caroline Ingraham Lee, Woon Hyang Jung, Sarah Charmoli, James Montgomery, Mary F. Gurton, Christine Thompson, Joy E. Allen, Elizabeth Hamilton, Bella Vendramini, Stephen Hill, Anthony C. Ranville, Jessica Leigh, Janice Berkowitz, Steve London, Elizabeth Forst, Zoe Bell, Anthony Wong, Douglas L. Farr, Maria Teresa Armijos Burneo, Lindsay Sanders, Sarah R. Carroll, Mark Thielen, David Poznanter, Matthew Schildkret, Branden Peak, Cynthia A. Peyton, Paul Tacorian, Henry Pope, Christine Lenick, Sander Zegveld, Lauren J. Law, Sarah Engelhart, Barbara T. Ryan, Marcella Fredericks, David E. Lewis, Raul Gasteazoro, Estela Sanchez, Julian McMorrow, Garron Chang, Joanne Davidson, Jessica Acosta, Jessie S. Hochberg, Benny Parkes, Florante Sarmiento, Carol A. Peringer, Randi Mohilner, Wilma J. McMorrow, Rebecca Ueno, Eileen R. Duncan, Melanie Wrenshall, Laura Staton, Linda L. Ginn, Lori A. Bennett, David Rose, Gilbert Rochecouste, Egil Aslak Hagerup, Anusha Wijeyakumar, Samuel Wehrmeyer, Andy Shrader, David King, V. B. Fassbender, Kyle

Bonis, John Mazlish, Nicole Landers, Samuel A. Margolius, Aria McLauchlan, Mariana Novak, Mark Shapiro, Dafna Laurie, Brittney Banks, Mariana Foreman, Chance Foreman, Amy Holster Phillips, Erica Corbett, Daniel N. Johnson, Phillip Glau, Clare Willison, Catherine Davidson, Elaine Browne, Tish Bell, Mary E. Johnston, Suze Q. Pirnat, Claire M. Jurs, Anna McLaren, Phaitoon Sarujikamjornwattana, Carielle Doe, Linda Loo, Catalina Yang, Andrew Glickman, Joe Clark, David C. Sloane, Mona Holmes, Daiva Anu, Lisa Faiman, Jill Bresnahan, Charlene Peterson, Christian Spreitz, Mathew Gerson, Sanjay Sabarwal, Kevin Lee, Glenn T. McMorrow, Shawn Greenbaum, Richard A. Adamski, Kent D. Phillips, Ed Wilkerson, Libby Wilkerson, L. DeKoven Ashley, Heidi Duran, Tao Luo, Sean Gray, Thomas Erba, Kelly Ford, Evan Corey, Lindsay Benner, Paul S. Henriques, Alex Cooper, Samantha Wilkerson, Eduardo Manilla, Paul R. Sitter, Rob Herring, Peter Harding, Matthew C. Schwartz, R. M. Dean, Alicia Henry, Cheryl J. Marshall, Katherine Kelly, Kristen Beckerdite, Jonathan Pellish, Alexandra L. Heyneman, C. Elizaga, Cheryl A. Nolan, Nicole Granato, Douglas M. Abrams, Maria Selma Jones, Garrett Cornelison, Simone Ubaldi, Lauren Quan-Madrid, Alexander Aboshiha, Martin Dru, Mandy C. Swann, Abigail Myers, Ken Masterton, Sarah Wright, Andrew McGregor, Christine Jacobs, Lori Ann Pennington, Steven C. Moss, Frank Tamborello, Jannika Kremer, Andrea Shapiro, John Seravic, Kathleen Fagan, Sabrina Elizondo, Elena Astilleros, Kelly Stewart, Cheri Johnson, Kay Cervantes, Sammy Gomez, Tyree N. Dillingham, Bob Erlenbusch, Julian McMorrow, Lauren Noel, Diane Capaldi, Tyler Newman, Alicia Yaffe, Jessica Ortega, Azzurro Mallin, Caitlin A. Hawley, Ximena Mutis, Vivian C. Wang, Ashton Watkins, Kevin McKeown, Katie Randall, Jenna Phillips, Connie Tsai, Sanjay Sabarwal, Mary Halls, Izzy Kirkby, Judit Seid, Praveen Kathpal, Beth Lynch, Enxia Zhang, Michael Saez, Christina T. McMorrow, Kennedy L. Thompson, Saleem Kalla, Justin P. Ma, Justin Scoggins, Jered S. Hughes, Glenda

L. Leister, Jo Pointer, Todd Hannigan, Patrick O'Brien Murphy, Brooke Black, Cheryll Lynn, Catina Gordon, Luke Craig, and Joseph Melville, as well as filmmakers Sophia Savage, Fortunato Procopio, Loren Graves, and Sam Gordon.

Deep bow to all that is, and the interconnectedness of all things.

NOTES

EPIGRAPH

1. Jalal al-Din Rumi, *Rumi: The Book of Love: Poems of Ecstasy and Longing*, trans. Coleman Barks (New York: Harper Collins, 2003).

INTRODUCTION

1. Katharine Wilkinson, "How Empowering Women and Girls Can Help Stop Global Warming," filmed November 2018 at TED Women 2018, video, 13:40, ted.com/talks/katharine_wilkinson _how_empowering_women_and_girls_can_help_stop _global_warming.

2. T. S. Eliot, "Little Gidding," *Four Quartets* (New York: Houghton Mifflin Harcourt, 1971).

3. "Why Do We Speak of '4 Per 1000?'" 4 Pour 1000, 4p1000.org.

4. Linda Sivertsen, Beautiful Writers Group coaching call, August 2015.

5. Danielle LaPorte, Linda Sivertsen, and Marianne Williamson, "From Tears to Triumph," June 24, 2016, in *Beautiful Writers Podcast*, 44:22, podcasts.apple.com/us/podcast/marianne-williamson-from -tears-to-triumph/id1047012231?i=1000371314460.

CHAPTER 1: IMAGINE THE YEAR 2050

1. "NOAA-led Researchers Discover Ocean Acidity Is Dissolving Shells of Tiny Snails off the U.S. West Coast," National Oceanic and Atmospheric Administration: U.S. Department of Commerce, April 30, 2014, noaa.gov/noaa-led-researchers-discover-ocean -acidity-dissolving-shells-tiny-snails-us-west-coast.

2. Richard Spinrad and Ian Boyd, "Our Deadened, Carbon-Soaked Seas," *New York Times*, October 15, 2015, nytimes.com/2015/10/16 /opinion/our-deadened-carbon-soaked-seas.html?_r=0.

3. Carol Turley, "Ocean Acidification," updated April 2020, noaa.gov /education/resource-collections/ocean-coasts/ocean-acidification.

4. Michael Mann, "Earth Will Cross the Climate Threshold by 2036," *Scientific American*, April 1, 2014, scientificamerican.com/article /earth-will-cross-the-climate-danger-threshold-by-2036/.

5. Chelsea Harvey, "Climate Change is Becoming a Top Threat to Biodiversity," *Scientific American*, March 28, 2018, scientificamerican.com/article/climate-change-is-becoming -a-top-threat-to-biodiversity/.

6. "Desertification: The Invisible Frontline," United Nations Convention to Combat Desertification, December 11, 2014, unccd.int/sites/default/files/documents/12112014_Invisible %20frontline_ENG.pdf.

7. National Aeronautics and Space Administration (NASA), "As Earth Warms, NASA Targets 'Other Half' of Carbon, Climate Equation," press release, November 12, 2015, nasa.gov/press-release/as-earth -warms-nasa-targets-other-half-of-carbon-climate-equation/.

8. NASA, "As Earth Warms, NASA Targets 'Other Half' of Carbon, Climate Equation."

9. Todd Ontl and Lisa Schulte, "Soil Carbon Storage," *Nature Education Knowledge* 3, no. 10 (2102): 35, nature.com/scitable /knowledge/library/soil-carbon-storage-84223790/.

10. Anodea Judith, *Eastern Body, Western Mind: Psychology and the Chakra System as a Path to the Self* (Berkeley: Celestial Arts, 2004).

11. Gerardo Ceballos, Paul Ehrlich, and Rodolfo Dirzo, "Biological Annihilation via the Ongoing Sixth Mass Extinction Signaled by Vertebrate Population Losses and Declines," *Proceedings of the National Academy of Sciences of the United States*, 114, no. 30 (July 10, 2017): e6089–e6096, doi.org/10.1073/pnas.1704949114.

12. Lauren Morello, "Phytoplankton Population Drops 40 Percent Since 1950," *Scientific American*, July 29, 2010, scientificamerican .com/article/phytoplankton-population/.

13. David Biello, "400 PPM: Carbon Dioxide in the Atmosphere Reaches Prehistoric Levels," *Scientific American*, May 9, 2013, blogs.scientificamerican.com/observations/2013/05/09/400-ppm -carbon-dioxide-in-the-atmosphere-reaches-prehistoric-levels/.

14. Mann, "Earth Will Cross the Climate Threshold by 2036."

CHAPTER 2: THE LEGACY LOAD

1. Brian Kahn, "Earth's CO2 Passes the 400 PPM Threshold—
   Maybe Permanently," *Scientific American*, September 27, 2016,
   scientificamerican.com/article/earth-s-co2-passes-the-400-ppm
   -threshold-maybe-permanently/.

2. Intergovernmental Panel on Climate Change (IPCC), *Fifth
   Assessment Report*, October 2014, ipcc.ch/assessment-report/ar5/.

3. IPCC, *Fifth Assessment Report*.

4. "NOAA-led Researchers Discover Ocean Acidity is Dissolving
   Shells of Tiny Snails off the U.S. West Coast," National Oceanic
   and Atmospheric Administration: U.S. Department of Commerce,
   April 30, 2014, noaa.gov/noaa-led-researchers-discover-ocean
   -acidity-dissolving-shells-tiny-snails-us-west-coast.

5. J. E. N. Veron, "Mass Extinctions and Ocean Acidification:
   Biological Constraints on Geological Dilemmas," *Coral Reefs* 27,
   no. 3 (September 2008): 459–472, doi.org/10.1007
   /s00338-008-0381-8.

CHAPTER 3: THE STORY OF ALL THINGS

1. Ron Sender, Shai Fuchs, and Ron Milo, "Revised Estimates for the
   Number of Human and Bacteria Cells in the Human Body," *PLOS
   Biology* 14, no. 8 (August 19, 2016): e1002533, ncbi.nlm.nih.gov
   /pmc/articles/PMC4991899/.

2. Nadia Drake, "This May Be the Oldest Known Sign of Life on
   Earth," *National Geographic*, March 1, 2017, nationalgeographic
   .com/news/2017/03/oldest-life-earth-iron-fossils-canada-vents
   -science/.

3. "Cyanobacteria: Life History and Ecology," UCMP Berkeley,
   ucmp.berkeley.edu/bacteria/cyanolh.html.

4. H. Eswaran, R. Lal, and P. F. Reich, "Land Degradation: An
   Overview," republished by the USDA's Natural Resources
   Conservation Service Soils website, nrcs.usda.gov/wps/portal
   /nrcs/detail/soils/use/?cid=nrcs142p2_054028.

5. Intergovernmental Panel on Climate Change (IPCC), *Fifth
   Assessment Report*, October 2014, ipcc.ch/assessment-report/ar5/.

6. Melissa Gallant, "The Dirt on Soil Carbon," Ecosystem Marketplace,
   February 27, 2018, ecosystemmarketplace.com/articles/dirt
   -soil-carbon/.

7. Judith D. Schwartz, *Cows Save the Planet: And Other Improbable Ways of Restoring Soil to Heal the Earth* (White River Junction, VT: Chelsea Green Publishing, 2013), 39.

8. Schwartz, *Cows Save the Planet*, 22.

9. Paul Stamets, ed., *Fantastic Fungi: How Mushrooms Can Heal, Shift Consciousness, and Save the Planet* (San Rafael, CA: Earth Aware, 2019).

10. Bill Bryson, *A Short History of Nearly Everything* (New York: Broadway Books, 2004).

11. Schwartz, *Cows Save the Planet*, 34.

12. Matt Ridley, *Genome: The Autobiography of a Species in 23 Chapters* (New York: Harper Perennial, 2000).

13. Lara Bryant, "Organic Matter Can Improve Your Soil's Water Holding Capacity," blog on NRDC web page, May 27, 2015, nrdc.org/experts/lara-bryant/organic-matter-can-improve-your -soils-water-holding-capacity.

14. David Roberts, "'Brutal Logic' and Climate Communications," Grist, December 17, 2011, grist.org/climate-change/2011-12-16 -brutal-logic-and-climate-communications/.

PART TWO

1. Jalal al-Din Rumi, *Rumi: In The Arms of the Beloved,* trans. Jonathan Star (New York: Tarcher/Putnam, 1997).

CHAPTER 5: THE CRY OF ALL WOMEN

1. Matt Ridley, *Genome: The Autobiography of a Species in 23 Chapters* (New York: Harper Perennial, 2000).

2. Jeff Lieberman, "Science and Spirituality," TEDx Cambridge, YouTube video, 14:24, January 19, 2012, youtube.com /watch?v=N0--_R6xThs.

3. While I am moved by the message of this book, I do not condone the author's use of the word *Negroid* to describe any of the grandmothers. This term is an unfortunate result of the racist beginnings of the field of anthropology and no longer has a place in acceptable language.

4. Jennifer Barker Woolger and Roger Woolger, *The Goddess Within: A Guide to the Eternal Myths that Shape Women's Lives* (New York: Ballantine, 1989).

5. Chani Nicholas, *Goddess Wisdom: An Exploration of the Power of the Goddess in Your Chart: Part I: Vesta and Juno*, educational course offered in 2018.

6. Naomi Wolf, "The Brain Science of the Vagina Heralds a New Sexual Revolution," *The Guardian*, September 8, 2012, theguardian .com/commentisfree/2012/sep/08/brain-science-vagina-heralds -sexual-revolution.

CHAPTER 6: INNER WORK AND OUTER WORK ARE ONE

1. Jack Kerouac, *The Portable Jack Kerouac*, ed. Ann Charters (New York: Viking, 1995).

2. Allison Aubrey, "Forest Bathing: A Retreat to Nature Can Boost Immunity and Mood," NPR, July 17, 2017, npr.org/sections /health-shots/2017/07/17/536676954/forest-bathing-a-retreat -to-nature-can-boost-immunity-and-mood.

3. Stephen Levine with Ann Frederick, *Waking the Tiger: Healing Trauma* (Berkeley, CA: North Atlantic Books, 1997).

CHAPTER 8: WE ARE INHERENTLY WORTHY

1. Alyssa Nobriga, alyssanobriga.com.

2. Richard Rudd, *The Gene Keys: Embracing Your Higher Purpose* (London: Watkins, 2013).

3. Anodea Judith, *Eastern Body, Western Mind: Psychology and the Chakra System as a Path to the Self* (Berkeley: Celestial Arts, 2004).

CHAPTER 9: REMEMBERING WE ARE NATURE

1. "The Gut-Brain Connection," HEALTHbeat newsletter, Harvard Medical School, health.harvard.edu/diseases-and-conditions /the-gut-brain-connection.

CHAPTER 11: LIVING A REGENERATIVE LIFE

1. Michael Pollan, *In Defense of Food: An Eater's Manifesto* (New York: Penguin Press, 2008).

CHAPTER 12: OWNING OUR POWER

1. Tom Kenyon and Judi Sion, *The Magdalen Manuscript: The Alchemies of Horus & the Sex Magic of Isis* (Orcas, WA: ORB Communications, 2006).

2. Pam Grossman, *Waking the Witch: Reflections on Women, Magic, and Power* (New York: Gallery, 2019).

CHAPTER 13: WHAT'S POSSIBLE

1. Organic Trade Association, "Organic Industry Survey," 2019, ota.com/resources/organic-industry-survey.
2. Abraham H. Maslow, *Religions, Values, and Peak Experiences* (Columbus: Ohio State University Press, 1964).

CHAPTER 14: THE DIVINE DANCE

1. I learned this from the phenomenal Kundalini yoga instructor Suze-Q. Pirnat.

ABOUT THE AUTHOR

Erin Yu-Juin McMorrow, PhD, earned her doctorate in policy, planning, and development from the University of Southern California, studied political and social thought at the University of Virginia, and served as the director of housing policy with the Los Angeles Coalition to End Hunger and Homelessness. She is also a certified yoga teacher, craniosacral therapist, and entrepreneur living in Los Angeles. For more, visit erinmcmorrow.com.

ABOUT SOUNDS TRUE

Sounds True is a multimedia publisher whose mission is to inspire and support personal transformation and spiritual awakening. Founded in 1985 and located in Boulder, Colorado, we work with many of the leading spiritual teachers, thinkers, healers, and visionary artists of our time. We strive with every title to preserve the essential "living wisdom" of the author or artist. It is our goal to create products that not only provide information to a reader or listener but also embody the quality of a wisdom transmission.

For those seeking genuine transformation, Sounds True is your trusted partner. At SoundsTrue.com you will find a wealth of free resources to support your journey, including exclusive weekly audio interviews, free downloads, interactive learning tools, and other special savings on all our titles.

To learn more, please visit SoundsTrue.com/freegifts or call us toll-free at 800.333.9185.